# LOUIS A**

Best known for his theories of ideology and its impact on politics and culture, Louis Althusser revolutionized Marxist theory. His writing changed the face of literary and cultural studies and continues to influence political modes of criticism such as feminism, post-colonialism and queer theory.

Beginning with an introduction to the crucial context of Marxist theory, this book goes on to explain:

- How Althusser interpreted and developed Marx's work
- The political implications of reading
- Ideology and its significance for culture and criticism
- Althusser's aesthetic theories of literature, theatre and art

Placing Althusser's key ideas in the context of earlier Marxist thought, as well as tracing their development and impact, Luke Ferretter provides a wide-ranging yet accessible guide, ideal for those new to the work of this influential critical thinker.

**Luke Ferretter** is a Sesqui Postdoctoral Research Fellow in English at the University of Sydney.

# ROUTLEDGE CRITICAL THINKERS

Series Editor: Robert Eaglestone, Royal Holloway, University of London

*Routledge Critical Thinkers* is a series of accessible introductions to key figures in contemporary critical thought.

With a unique focus on historical and intellectual contexts, each volume examines a key theorist's:

- significance
- motivation
- key ideas and their sources
- impact on other thinkers

Concluding with extensively annotated guides to further reading, *Routledge Critical Thinkers* are the student's passport to today's most exciting critical thought.

Already available:

*Louis Althusser* by Luke Ferretter
*Roland Barthes* by Graham Allen
*Jean Baudrillard* by Richard J. Lane
*Simone de Beauvoir* by Ursula Tidd
*Maurice Blanchot* by Ullrich Haase and William Large
*Judith Butler* by Sara Salih
*Gilles Deleuze* by Claire Colebrook
*Jacques Derrida* by Nicholas Royle
*Michel Foucault* by Sara Mills
*Sigmund Freud* by Pamela Thurschwell
*Stuart Hall* by James Procter
*Martin Heidegger* by Timothy Clark

*Fredric Jameson* by Adam Roberts
*Jean-François Lyotard* by Simon Malpas
*Jacques Lacan* by Sean Homer
*Julia Kristeva* by Noëlle McAfee
*Paul de Man* by Martin McQuillan
*Friedrich Nietzsche* by Lee Spinks
*Paul Ricoeur* byKarl Simms
*Edward Said* by Bill Ashcroft and Pal Ahluwalia
*Gayatri Chakravorty Spivak* by Stephen Morton
*Slavoj Žižek* by Tony Myers

For further details on this series, see www.literature.routledge.com/literature

# LOUIS ALTHUSSER

*Luke Ferretter*

LONDON AND NEW YORK

First published 2006
by Routledge
2 Park Square, Milton Park, Abingdon, Oxford, OX14 4RN

Simultaneously published in the USA and Canada
by Routledge
270 Madison Ave, New York, NY 10016

*Routledge is an imprint of the Taylor & Francis Group*

© 2006 Luke Ferretter

Typeset in Perpetua by
Taylor & Francis Books
Printed and bound in Great Britain by
Antony Rowe Ltd, Chippenham, Wiltshire

All rights reserved. No part of this book may be reprinted
or reproduced or utilised in any form or by any electronic,
mechanical, or other means, now known or hereafter
invented, including photocopying and recording, or in any
information storage or retrieval system, without permission in
writing from the publishers.

*British Library Cataloguing in Publication Data*
A catalogue record for this book is available from the British Library

*Library of Congress Cataloging in Publication Data*
A catalog record for this book has been requested

ISBN10: 0-415-32731-8     ISBN13: 978-0-415-32731-2 (hbk)
ISBN10: 0-415-32732-6     ISBN13: 978-0-415-32732-9 (pbk)

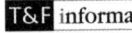

Taylor & Francis Group is the Academic Division of T&F Informa plc.

**FOR PETER**

# CONTENTS

| | |
|---|---|
| Series editor's preface | viii |
| Acknowledgements | xii |

## WHY ALTHUSSER?     1

## KEY IDEAS     9

| | | |
|---|---|---|
| 1 | The cornerstones: Marx and the theory of culture | 11 |
| 2 | The revolution in theory: Althusser's Marxism | 27 |
| 3 | The politics of reading: essays on interpretation | 51 |
| 4 | The politics of culture: essays on ideology | 75 |
| 5 | Materialist aesthetics: essays on literature and art | 95 |
| 6 | Posthumous confessions: *The Future Lasts a Long Time* | 111 |

## AFTER ALTHUSSER     123

## FURTHER READING     145

| | |
|---|---|
| Works Cited | 155 |
| Index | 159 |

# SERIES EDITOR'S PREFACE

The books in this series offer introductions to major critical thinkers who have influenced literary studies and the humanities. The *Routledge Critical Thinkers* series provides the books you can turn to first when a new name or concept appears in your studies.

Each book will equip you to approach a key thinker's original texts by explaining her or his key ideas, putting them into context and, perhaps most importantly, showing you why this thinker is considered to be significant. The emphasis is on concise, clearly written guides which do not presuppose a specialist knowledge. Although the focus is on particular figures, the series stresses that no critical thinker ever existed in a vacuum but, instead, emerged from a broader intellectual, cultural and social history. Finally, these books will act as a bridge between you and the thinker's original texts: not replacing them but rather complementing what she or he wrote.

These books are necessary for a number of reasons. In his 1997 autobiography, *Not Entitled*, the literary critic Frank Kermode wrote of a time in the 1960s:

> On beautiful summer lawns, young people lay together all night, recovering from their daytime exertions and listening to a troupe of Balinese musicians. Under their blankets or their sleeping bags, they would chat drowsily about

> the gurus of the time ... What they repeated was largely hearsay; hence my lunchtime suggestion, quite impromptu, for a series of short, very cheap books offering authoritative but intelligible introductions to such figures.

There is still a need for 'authoritative and intelligible introductions'. But this series reflects a different world from the 1960s. New thinkers have emerged and the reputations of others have risen and fallen, as new research has developed. New methodologies and challenging ideas have spread through the arts and humanities. The study of literature is no longer – if it ever was – simply the study and evaluation of poems, novels and plays. It is also the study of the ideas, issues, and difficulties which arise in any literary text and in its interpretation. Other arts and humanities subjects have changed in analogous ways.

With these changes, new problems have emerged. The ideas and issues behind these radical changes in the humanities are often presented without reference to wider contexts or as theories which you can simply 'add on' to the texts you read. Certainly, there's nothing wrong with picking out selected ideas or using what comes to hand – indeed, some thinkers have argued that this is, in fact, all we can do. However, it is sometimes forgotten that each new idea comes from the pattern and development of somebody's thought and it is important to study the range and context of their ideas. Against theories 'floating in space', the *Routledge Critical Thinkers* series places key thinkers and their ideas firmly back in their contexts.

More than this, these books reflect the need to go back to the thinker's own texts and ideas. Every interpretation of an idea, even the most seemingly innocent one, offers its own 'spin', implicitly or explicitly. To read only books on a thinker, rather than texts by that thinker, is to deny yourself a chance of making up your own mind. Sometimes what makes a significant figure's work hard to approach is not so much its style or content as the feeling of not knowing where to start. The purpose of these books is to give you a 'way in' by offering an accessible overview of these thinkers' ideas and works and by guiding your further reading, starting with each thinker's own texts. To use a metaphor from the philosopher Ludwig Wittgenstein (1889-1951), these books are ladders, to be thrown away after you have climbed to the next level. Not only, then, do they equip you to approach new ideas, but also they empower you, by leading you back to a theorist's own texts and encouraging you to develop your own informed opinions.

Finally, these books are necessary because, just as intellectual needs have changed, the education systems around the world – the contexts in which introductory books are usually read – have changed radically, too. What was suitable for the minority higher education system of the 1960s is not suitable for the larger, wider, more diverse, high technology education systems of the twenty-first century. These changes call not just for new, up-to-date, introductions but new methods of presentation. The presentational aspects of *Routledge Critical Thinkers* have been developed with today's students in mind.

Each book in the series has a similar structure. They begin with a section offering an overview of the life and ideas of each thinker and explain why she or he is important. The central section of each book discusses the thinker's key ideas, their context, evolution and reception. Each book concludes with a survey of the thinker's impact, outlining how their ideas have been taken up and developed by others. In addition, there is a detailed final section suggesting and describing books for further reading. This is not a 'tacked-on' section but an integral part of each volume. In the first part of this section you will find brief descriptions of the thinker's key works, then, following this, information on the most useful critical works and, in some cases, on relevant websites. This section will guide you in your reading, enabling you to follow your interests and develop your own projects. Throughout each book, references are given in what is known as the Harvard system (the author and the date of a work cited are given in the text and you can look up the full details in the bibliography at the back). This offers a lot of information in very little space. The books also explain technical terms and use boxes to describe events or ideas in more detail, away from the main emphasis of the discussion. Boxes are also used at times to highlight definitions of terms frequently used or coined by a thinker. In this way, the boxes serve as a kind of glossary, easily identified when flicking through the book.

The thinkers in the series are 'critical' for three reasons. First, they are examined in the light of subjects which involve criticism: principally literary studies or English and cultural studies, but also other disciplines which rely on the criticism of books, ideas, theories and unquestioned assumptions. Second, they are critical because studying their work will provide you with a 'tool kit' for your own informed critical reading and thought, which will make you critical. Third, these thinkers are critical because they are crucially important: they deal with ideas and questions which can overturn conventional understandings of the world, of texts, of everything we take for granted, leaving us with a deeper understanding of what we already knew and with new ideas.

No introduction can tell you everything. However, by offering a way into critical thinking, this series hopes to begin to engage you in an activity which is productive, constructive and potentially life-changing.

# ACKNOWLEDGEMENTS

I was enabled to begin work on this book by a British Academy Postdoctoral Fellowship. I should like to thank the President and Fellows of Wolfson College, Cambridge, for the award of a Junior Research Fellowship, and Stefan Collini and Claire Daunton for making my time at the Cambridge English Faculty so productive. I should also like to thank the Research Office and the School of English, Art History, Film and Media at the University of Sydney for the award of a Sesqui Postdoctoral Research Fellowship, during whose tenure this book was written. Adrian Mitchell and Tony Miller ran a school and department that could not have been more conducive to research.

I could not have written this book without the support of my parents and parents-in-law, for which I continue to thank them. Special thanks to Bob Eaglestone, for his continued and productive support of the project, and to Liz Thompson for her professional and constructive editorship. Finally, my wife Jen made everything about this book possible. I dedicate it to my son Peter, *mobilis in mobili*.

Extracts from the following works are reprinted by permission of Verso: Louis Althusser, *For Marx*, trans. Ben Brewster (London, 1969); Louis Althusser, *Lenin and Philosophy, and Other Essays*, trans. Ben Brewster (London, 1971).

For a list of abbreviations used in references to Althusser's works in this book, please see the Works Cited section. All italics in quotations are original.

# WHY ALTHUSSER?

The short answer to the question 'Why Althusser?' must be 'Because of capitalism'. As long as we live in a society based on a capitalist economy, in which goods are produced in order to be sold at a profit, we will not be able to understand the literature and culture of that society without thinkers like Althusser. Let me begin with an example. In Richard Attenborough's film *Chaplin* (1992), Charlie Chaplin (Robert Downey Jr) and Douglas Fairbanks Jr (Kevin Kline) ride up into the Hollywood Hills to the famous Hollywood sign. It then read 'Hollywoodland', originally an advertisement for a real estate development. Fairbanks is worried about Chaplin – an FBI agent has visited him, asking if everyone in his circle is a 'loyal American'. He asked if Chaplin was a member of the Communist Party. Fairbanks advises Chaplin to be careful in this authoritarian climate:

Fairbanks: You're a foreigner, you're still an outsider. You've never understood this country.
Chaplin: It's a good country underneath, Doug.
Fairbanks: No – it's a good country on top. Underneath – that's what starts showing when we're scared.

To call a country 'good on top' but less good in reality is to point to what the Marxist tradition describes as 'ideology'. This term has a complex history, but what is meant by it is essentially this. Capitalism is a system of exploitation. It depends in numerous ways on the exploitation of certain classes of human beings by others. The suffering of the industrial working class described in Friedrich Engels' *The Condition of the Working Class in England* (1844) is just one historical example of the fact that, for one social class to benefit from the profits of a capitalist economy, another must live in poverty and misery. How do we justify living on the basis of such a system to ourselves? Put simply, by never speaking of it as such. In all our discourses, Marxists argue, from economic theory and philosophy to novels and news reports, we systematically misrepresent the reality of the socio-economic relationships in which we live. This politically motivated misrepresentation is what is meant by 'ideology'. For Althusser, it occurs in all the many ways in which we use language in capitalist society, including literature, mass culture, and our critical responses to these discourses. Attenborough's film suggests as much: Douglas Fairbanks describes his country as 'good on top' as he sits on the Hollywood sign, symbolizing the culture industry. Unlike Chaplin, Althusser was a member of the Communist Party. He revolutionized Marxist theory, especially the theory of ideology. For all of us who live in a society that is good on top, Althusser shows us how to make sense of the literature and the culture we produce and read in that society. It is only on the basis of this kind of understanding, he argues, that we can contribute to changing it.

## ALTHUSSER'S LIFE

Louis Pierre Althusser was born in October 1918 near Algiers, the eldest son of a bank manager and a former schoolteacher. He grew up in Algiers, and also in France, in Marseille and Lyon. A devout Catholic, he founded a student Christian movement and even considered a religious vocation. In September 1939 he passed the entrance examination to the prestigious École normale supérieure in Paris, in which university teachers are trained, but he was called up before he could begin his studies. He became a prisoner of war in June 1940. Transported to a prison camp in northern Germany, he was initially assigned to hard labour, but after falling ill, worked as a nurse in the camp infirmary. This gave him the time to read widely in philosophy and literature. After the liberation, he took up his studies at the École normale, writing a master's thesis in 1947 on the German idealist philosopher G.W.F. Hegel (1770–1831). In 1948 he was made tutor in philosophy, and remained at the École normale supérieure for the rest of his career. Although he maintained his Catholic faith for several years after the war, he joined the Communist Party in October 1948, a move made by many French intellectuals of the period. As Althusser wrote in an autobiographical text, 'Communism was in the air in 1945, after the German defeat, the victory at Stalingrad, and the hopes and lessons of the Resistance' (*FLLT*: 339). He continued this uneasy dual membership of the mutually hostile Catholic Church and Communist Party for longer than he publicly admitted, probably until the early 1950s, when the Vatican prohibited Catholics from membership in the worker-priest movement and other radical organizations, in the value of which Althusser had strongly believed. From 1960, Althusser began a series of highly influential studies on the philosophy of Karl Marx (1818–1883), which he published in 1965 under the title *For Marx*. Against the current trend to integrate Marx's work into contemporary systems of thought, including Catholicism, Althusser insisted that Marx had founded a radically new science, incommensurable with all non-Marxist thought. From 1960–1966, he expounded the fundamental principles of this science, of which he argued that Marx had 'left us the cornerstones'. One contemporary reviewer described his project as follows:

> A new generation of rebels requires a new version of revolutionary ideology, and M. Althusser is essentially an ideological hard-liner, challenging the political and intellectual softening around him.
>
> (Hobsbawm 1994: 4)

In the same year as *For Marx* was published (1965), *Reading Capital* appeared, a series of papers on Marx's *Capital* (first published in 1867 as *Das Kapital*) written by Althusser and a group of his students at the École normale supérieure. In this book, I will devote considerable attention to the work of one of these students, Pierre Macherey (b. 1938), since it was he who followed through in greatest detail the logic of Althusser's thought in the fields of literary theory and criticism. From 1967, following criticism from the Communist Party and in the light of developments in the international Communist movement, Althusser recanted some of his earlier positions. He renounced the 'theoreticism' of his earlier work, by which he meant his emphasis on the meaning of Marx's work in theoretical discourse. In its place, he aimed to put the class struggle at the forefront of his work. Hence he defined philosophy as 'the class struggle in theory'.

Althusser suffered seriously from bi-polar disorder – periods of severe depression, followed by manic phases – throughout his life. In 1976 he estimated that he had spent fifteen of the previous thirty years in hospitals and psychiatric clinics. From 1963, he underwent regular psychoanalysis, a practice of whose therapeutic value he was profoundly convinced, and in which he took a detailed theoretical interest. In November 1980, following the worst of his depressions, Althusser strangled his wife and companion of over thirty years, Hélène Rytmann (also known as Hélène Legotien), a sociologist and former member of the Resistance. Amid much public controversy, he was declared unfit to plead to the crime, on the grounds that his mental state rendered him irresponsible for his actions. He spent the next three years, and most of the rest of his life, in psychiatric hospitals, his public career as a teacher and writer over. He continued to write during the last ten years of his life, and his philosophical thought continued to develop. He published a series of interviews with the Mexican philosopher Fernanda Navarro in Mexico in 1988. After his death in October 1990, tens of thousands of pages of unpublished material, including some ten books, were discovered in his archive. The text that has attracted most attention among this material has been *The Future Lasts a Long Time*, the psychological autobiography Althusser wrote in 1985 in place of the testimony he would have given concerning the murder of his wife had he been judged fit to plead to the crime.

## ALTHUSSER'S WORK: AN OVERVIEW

Althusser's work can be broadly divided into five periods:

1   1946–51: Early Work. Althusser articulates a complex transition from Hegelianism to Marxism, and from Catholicism to Communism.

Some of the major pieces from this period are collected in *The Spectre of Hegel* (1997).

2  1960–66: Marxist Revolution in Theory. The 'high' period of Althusser's work – a period of intense productivity, in which he expounds the fundamental propositions of the science of history discovered by Marx. Althusser's best-known works from this period are *For Marx* (1965) and *Reading Capital* (1965).

3  1967–75: Self-criticism. Althusser renounces the theoretical emphasis of his earlier work, and defines philosophy as 'the class struggle in theory'. The major works of this period are 'Philosophy and the Spontaneous Philosophy of the Scientists' (1967) and the essays collected in *Lenin and Philosophy* (1971) and *Essays in Self-Criticism* (1976).

4  1976–78: The Crisis of Marxism. Althusser criticizes Communist Party theory and practice with increasing bitterness, calling for a self-critical re-interpretation of the work of Marx. The major essays of this period are 'On the 22nd Congress of the French Communist Party' (1977), 'The Crisis of Marxism' (1977), 'What Must Change in the Party' (1978) and 'Marxism Today' (1978).

5  1982–88: 'Aleatory Materialism'. The first term means 'concerning chance'. Aleatory materialism is a philosophy of history that, unlike historical materialism, takes the concept of chance into account. In fragmentary texts and interviews, Althusser argues that history is not a necessary process, in the sense that Marxism has always claimed, but the result of a series of accidental encounters. The main texts from this period are 'Le courant souterrain du matérialisme de la rencontre' ('The Underground Current of Materialism of the Encounter'), written in 1982, and *Sur la philosophie* ('On Philosophy'), published posthumously in French in 1994. At the time of writing, these texts have not been translated, but an English introduction to them can be found in Navarro 1998.

In this book, we will focus on the second, third and fourth of these periods, although the final chapter will be devoted to a post-1980 text. Althusser continually asserted that his work was an interpretation – the only authentic interpretation among a host of misunderstandings – of the work of Karl Marx, and so we will begin with an examination of the basic outlines of Marx's thought. In chapter 2 we will examine the principles of Althusser's Marxism, focusing on the significance of his theory of society for literary and cultural criticism. We will also situate his work in its contemporary contexts. This book emphasizes the significance of Althusser's work in literary and cultural studies, so in chapter 3 we will discuss the reading practice Althusser discovers in Marx's *Capital*, which he applies back to Marx's own work in order to generate his distinctive interpretation of this work. He calls this 'symptomatic reading', by analogy with a psychoanalyst's reading of the symptoms of her patient's discourse. We will examine in detail Pierre Macherey's application of this concept in literary criticism. Finally, we will discuss Althusser's later concept of philosophy as the class struggle in theory, emphasizing the new reading practice that this concept entails. In chapter 4 we will examine Althusser's contribution to the Marxist theory of ideology, which has been the most influential aspect of his work in literary and cultural studies. Chapter 5 discusses Althusser's own practice of cultural criticism, along with his essays in aesthetic theory. We will finish with an account of the extraordinary autobiography – *The Future Lasts a Long Time* – that Althusser wrote after the death of his wife, and which was published after his own death, emphasizing the relationship of this book to the philosophical body of work on which it reflects and from which it differs so considerably.

## ALTHUSSER IN LITERARY STUDIES

Althusser's work has been extremely influential in British and American literary and cultural criticism since the 1970s, the decade of the 'theory revolution' in literary studies. Indeed, it is partly from the thought of Althusser that the sense of the term 'theory', in disciplinary fields such as 'literary theory' and 'critical theory', derives. As the flowering of new philosophies in France in the 1960s filtered into English-speaking universities in the 1970s, Althusser's work – the most explicitly radical of these philosophies – offered literary critics the possibility of an entirely new kind of literary criticism. The critical orthodoxies that had prevailed since the 1930s – the elite sensibilities of F.R. Leavis and T.S. Eliot in Britain, and the rigorously textual New Criticism in the United States – had bracketed politics from literary analysis. Although there had been a Marxist tradition of criticism in these countries, it lacked intellectual rigour and knew it. Althusser offered British and American literary critics a revolutionary theory of society in whose terms literature could and should be understood, and a politically significant rationale for doing so. In the light of his work, it seemed that literary criticism could for the first time become both scientifically true and politically radical. Political theory and criticism have diversified and become more complex since the revolutionary excitement of literary studies in the 1970s. Nevertheless, if we are to understand the significance of contemporary forms of politically committed theory and criticism – of New Historicism and cultural materialism, of gay and queer theory, of race-oriented and post-colonial criticism, of feminist criticisms, of cultural studies, or of post-Marxism – it is essential to read and understand the work of Althusser, to which all of them are in various ways indebted.

# KEY IDEAS

# 1

# THE CORNERSTONES: MARX AND THE THEORY OF CULTURE

Althusser is a Marxist philosopher. The intention that governs all his major work is that Marx's thought and practice – with all that it means for the struggle of the working class – should be rightly understood and acted upon. When asked about 'Althusserian' theory in 1980, his former student and co-author Étienne Balibar responded that, strictly speaking, there is no such thing as Althusserian theory. As he replied to his interviewer, 'Althusser is not an "Althusserian". He is a Marxist' (Balibar and Macherey 1982: 46). Balibar was right. Although he underwent a journey towards Marxism in his very early work, and although he began to think outside its frame of reference in his very late work, during the period of his most influential thought (1960–80), Althusser was a Marxist philosopher. His work consisted entirely in understanding – in a situation in which he claimed it had been obscured or never properly understood in the first place – the immense theoretical revolution that had taken place in the work of Karl Marx. In order to make sense of Althusser's work, therefore, which he consistently claimed was an interpretation of Marx, we need to understand the basic elements of Marx's thought. In this chapter, I will outline these elements. We will discuss Marx's theory of human history, and his theory of the place of human discourses – that is, extended uses of language, from novels to newspapers – in society. Finally, we will deal with the question of the humanism of his early work, which is where Althusser's intervention begins.

## THE MATERIALIST CONCEPTION OF HISTORY

In *The German Ideology* (1845), Karl Marx and Friedrich Engels (1820–1895), his friend and intellectual co-worker for forty years, set out the basis of a new world-view. They called it the 'materialist conception of history'. *The German Ideology* was initially intended as a critique of the Young Hegelian school of radical philosophers and theologians, with whom Marx and Engels had until then been associated. As Marx wrote later, it was intended 'to settle accounts with our erstwhile philosophical conscience' (*SW*: 390). The Young Hegelians were materialist philosophers, best known for their subversive critique of religion. Most influential among them were Ludwig Feuerbach (1804–1872) and Bruno Bauer (1809–1882). Despite their apparently radical ideas, Marx and Engels argue that the Young Hegelians are in fact not radical enough, inasmuch as they think that human lives are governed by *ideas*. Their critique of religion, for example, was based on the premise that, once the religious misrepresentation of the world was abolished, men and women could begin to order their lives on the basis of a correct understanding of them. But however much the Young Hegelians may criticize a system of ideas, Marx and Engels object, the substitution only of another system of ideas will not in practice make the slightest difference to the real lives of the men and women they fancy themselves to be liberating. In fact, Marx and Engels write, their former comrades are 'the staunchest conservatives' (*GI*: 30), since it is not ideas at all but the *material conditions in which they live* from which people need liberation. Marx calls the Young Hegelians sheep in wolves' clothing, and likens them to men who believe that people drown because they have the idea of gravity in their heads. What drowning people need, of course, is not a different idea than that of gravity, but a lifebuoy.

If the Young Hegelians believe that they can change people's lives by changing their ideas, Marx and Engels begin from the opposite premise, that it is the material conditions in which people live that determine every aspect of their lives, including their ideas:

> The premises from which we begin are not arbitrary ones, not dogmas, but real premises, from which abstraction can be made only in the imagination. They are the real individuals, their activity and the material conditions of their life, both those which they find already existing and those produced by their activity.
>
> (*GI*: 31)

The first premise of all human history, for Marx and Engels, is the existence of living human individuals. The first fact to be understood about these individuals is that they organize themselves in relation to one another and to the natural world in which they find themselves. They distinguish themselves from other animals as soon as they begin to *produce* their means of subsistence out of the raw materials of nature. When men and women produce their means of subsistence in this way, according to Marx and Engels, they are 'indirectly producing their material life'. The way in which they do so is conditioned both by the form in which they have organized themselves and by the relation of this social organization to the natural environment:

> What [individuals] are, therefore, coincides with their production, both with *what* they produce and with *how* they produce. Hence what individuals are depends on the material conditions of their production.
>
> (*GI*: 31–32)

What Marx and Engels are saying – and this constitutes the first premise of the Marxist world-view, which Althusser intends correctly to expound – is that the first and fundamental fact of human life is not at all human ideas, whether the idea of God, of man, of the good, or whatever. Rather it is the forces and relations of production into which men and women enter in order to maintain and develop their material lives. By 'forces' of production, I mean the materials and the instruments of production, and by 'relations' of production, the way in which the members of a society are organized in order to produce their lives with these materials and instruments.

The materialist concepts of forces and relations of production are intended to displace all forms of idealist thought, or belief that the fundamental reality governing human life is an ideal, spiritual or non-tangible reality, like the soul, the spirit, the heart, or the personality. It is a cunning and exploitative myth, materialists hold, to claim that people have certain innate qualities that belong to each and every one of us as human beings – whether dignity, rights, freedom, humanity, or responsibilities. There is no *human nature*, they argue – no set of qualities I have as a human being (such as personality, humanity, morality, or the like) that would remain the same if I had lived in an altogether different set of material circumstances. If I were a Guatemalan coffee-picker or an Iranian housewife, I would be an altogether different human being than the one I am as a British literary scholar. This is not a question of privileging 'nurture' over 'nature' – genetics too is a materialist science. Rather, it is a claim that the material conditions in which a person lives are more than merely the circumstances or context of her life – they determine it in every way. If I am genetically coded to be intelligent, for example, but have to work in factory twelve hours a day from the time I am six, I will not be able to develop my intelligence in the way that a member of a different class or a different society does. Despite their banality, historically based reality TV shows such as *The Edwardian Country House* illustrate this point about forces and relations of production. To live in an aristocratic country house at the beginning of the twentieth century is to live an unrecognizably different life than to live in a middle-class suburb at the beginning of the twenty-first. Likewise, to live above stairs as a landed aristocrat is to live an unrecognizably different life from that experienced by a servant below stairs, even if the two are contemporaries. It is a person's place in the system by which society produces the material conditions of the lives of its members – and not any innate quality like humanity or personality – which determines their life in every respect. It is plainly false, materialists argue, to say that both the Edwardian aristocrats and their servants share their common humanity, that both groups have the freedom, dignity and rights proper to this humanity. It is clear, especially to the servants, that their lives are different in every way.

Marx sums up this materialist conception of history succinctly in a well-known passage from the preface to *A Critique of Political Economy* (1859):

> In the social production of their life, men enter into definite relations that are indispensable and independent of their will, relations of production which correspond to a definite stage of development of their material productive forces. The sum total of these relations of production constitutes the economic structure of society, the real foundation, on which rises a legal and political superstructure and to which correspond definite forms of social consciousness. The mode of production of material life conditions the social, political and intellectual life process in general. It is not the consciousness of men that determines their being, but, on the contrary, their social being that determines their consciousness.
>
> (SW: 389)

Here Marx goes on to explain a second fundamental principle of the materialist conception of history, namely that the sum total of the forces and relations of production in a given society constitutes its 'base' or 'infrastructure', which is its first and fundamental reality. Out of this economic base develops a 'superstructure', consisting of every other aspect of the life of that society. In the first place, the superstructure consists of the political and legal institutions according to which the society is structured – its constitution, its forms of government, its legal system, its judiciary, its defence systems and so on. In the second place, it consists of all the forms of consciousness in whose terms the members of society understand and represent themselves to each other, namely legal and political theories, philosophy, religion, art, literature, and every kind of cultural production. All these forms of consciousness comprise what Marx and Engels call 'ideology'. Marx thinks of the economic base of a society as the set of facts that determine the form of every element of the superstructure. For him, neither political formations nor legal institutions, nor any form of consciousness such as philosophy, religion or literature, exist or develop in themselves. Rather, they are determined and conditioned by the economic base – the forces and relations of production – of the society in which they appear. You do not only live a different life according to whether you wear Nike clothes or make them, pick Starbucks coffee or drink it – you also think differently and act differently. From the perspective of literary criticism, you also write differently.

## IDEOLOGY

Clearly, the literary and cultural products of a society, according to this view, are aspects of its ideology – that is, of the forms of consciousness in which its members represent their lives to one another in a way determined by that society's production relations. This is one of Marxism's major claims to significance for literary and cultural studies. According to the materialist conception of history, the meaning of literary and cultural works is to be found in their relationship to the economic base of the society that produced them. Marx and Engels make this clear in *The German Ideology*. They write that a systematic understanding of a society's intellectual and cultural products must be based on the understanding that these products are conditioned by the 'mode of production', or the sum total of the forces and relations of production, which constitutes that society's economic basis:

> It is a matter of ... setting out from real active men, and on the basis of their real life-process demonstrating the development of the ideological reflexes and echoes of this life-process. The phantoms formed in the brains of men are also, necessarily, sublimates of their material life-process.... Morality, religion, metaphysics, and all the rest of ideology as well as the forms of consciousness corresponding to these, thus no longer retain the semblance of independence. They have no history, no development; but men, developing their material production and their material intercourse, alter, along with this their actual world, also their thinking and the products of their thinking.
>
> (*GI*: 36–37)

Not only do men and women produce, in increasingly developed ways, their means of subsistence, for Marx and Engels, but they also produce their ideas, images and discourses. These cultural products are altogether determined by the more fundamental mode of production of means of subsistence arising from the society in which they appear.

The Marxist critic Fredric Jameson puts the materialist concept of ideology to work in his book *Postmodernism, or the Cultural Logic of Late Capitalism* (1991). As the title indicates, Jameson argues that all the aesthetic and cultural products we call postmodern – the fiction of Thomas Pynchon, the music of Philip Glass, the video art of Bill Viola, the screen prints of Andy Warhol, to name only some of the best-known genres – derive their characteristic qualities ultimately from the set of forces and relations of production which constitute the postmodern period (roughly, 1950 to the present). Analysing an example of postmodern architecture – John Portman's Westin Bonaventure Hotel in Los Angeles (1974–76) – Jameson argues that the experience of moving into, through and around the building is above all one of bewildered disorientation in the multiply complex environment that the building constitutes. He calls this environment 'hyperspace' because it explodes our ordinary perception of space. This experience of bewildered disorientation in an environment too complex for the individual to comprehend is a characteristic theme of postmodern culture – it is found in narratives of conspiracy theory, such as Pynchon's novel *Gravity's Rainbow* (1973), in cyberpunk science fiction like William Gibson's *Neuromancer* (1984), and in narratives of the Vietnam war such as Michael Herr's *Dispatches* (1977). Indeed, postmodern media themselves – the TV set, the TV camera, the TV network, the computer, the internet – involve networks of relationship that are too complex for the ordinary consumer of the cultural products they mediate to understand. Jameson argues that this postmodern motif of the incomprehensibly complex network, which the individual can neither understand nor control, is a cultural expression of the complex global network of economic relationships that constitute world capitalism at the turn of the twenty-first century:

> Our faulty representations of some immense communicational and computer network are themselves but a distorted figuration of something even

> deeper, namely, the whole world-system of a present-day multinational capitalism.
>
> (Jameson 1991: 37)

Postmodernism is, in Jameson's view, precisely what Marx and Engels describe as an ideology: the characteristic qualities of its aesthetic products derive from the forces and relations of production in the global, multinational, technological capitalist economy in which we live. This is what he means by describing it as the 'cultural logic of late capitalism'.

Now, production relations in society have never so far been arranged so that the means of subsistence and the material resources available to a society are equitably distributed among all its members. Relations of production have always been relations of *dominance* and of exploitation. As Marx and Engels put it in *The Communist Manifesto* (1848), 'The history of all hitherto existing society is the history of class struggles.' (*CM*: 219) This means that ideology has always been determined not just by production relations but by relations of class domination. As the set of ideas, images and discourses produced by a society whose mode of production is based on the exploitation of one class of its members by another, a society's ideology, like its material resources, is controlled by the ruling class and made to function in the interests of that class. Marx and Engels write:

> The ideas of the ruling class are in every epoch the ruling ideas: i.e., the class which is the ruling *material* force of society is at the same time its ruling *intellectual* force. The class which has the means of material production at its disposal, consequently also controls the means of mental production, so that the ideas of those who lack the means of mental production are on the whole subject to it. The ruling ideas are nothing more than the ideal expression of the dominant material relations ... hence of the relations which make the one class the ruling one.
>
> (*GI*: 59)

In Marx and Engels' view, then, ideology — including all the literary and cultural products which are a part of it — is a set of discourses whose function is to justify and maintain the position of the ruling class in a society that is based (as all societies have thus far been) on the economic exploitation of one class by another. It is a discourse of *class interest*. They give as an example of an ideological concept one which still resonates in public discourse today — that of 'freedom'. In mid-nineteenth century Britain, a high value was placed on the concept of individual freedom. Marx and Engels object that, in the industrial capitalism of nineteenth-century Britain, individual freedom was in fact only a property of the dominant classes, most powerful among which were the industrial capitalists. The mass of labourers who worked for this class had the 'freedom' only either to accept their low wages and long hours, or to starve. The individual freedom the bourgeoisie prized, although represented in its ideological discourses (from the newspapers to works of philosophy) as a natural and universal human right, was in fact the specific freedom to buy and sell without restriction, on which their economic dominance depended. The function of the ideology of freedom that they produced was precisely to justify and maintain this means of their dominance. This is what Marx and Engels mean in *The Communist Manifesto* when they respond to the claim of the middle classes that communism abolishes individual freedom:

> By freedom is meant, under the present bourgeois conditions of production, free trade, free selling and buying. ... Your very ideas are but the outgrowth of the conditions of your bourgeois production and bourgeois property.
> (*CM*: 237–38)

Jameson emphasizes this aspect of the ideology of postmodernism. The incomprehensibility of the contemporary world emphasized in postmodern literary and cultural works is an ideological motif in the sense that it serves the interest of the ruling economic classes. If the way in which society works can be kept incomprehensibly complex, then none of the disadvantaged majority of its members can formulate realistic ways of changing it. Disorientation is a desirable state in which to keep those your system exploits, because orientation within it is a precondition for ending their exploitation. The postmodern motif of the 'simulacrum' — the image which is not an image of any prior reality — functions in a similar way. In postmodern art and culture, Jameson argues, the image of reality becomes more real than reality itself. The commodified images of Andy Warhol, reality TV, and vast fantasy worlds like Disneyland or those Las Vegas hotels that have 'improved' upon Paris or Venice, are all examples of this culture of the simulacrum. If the eyes of the postmodern consumer are continually kept on a vast glossy image of reality that has developed the function precisely of substituting for reality (rather than of reflecting reality, as Shakespeare believed when he said that the function of art is to 'hold up the mirror to nature'), then whatever the mysterious nature of reality is, the consumer neither knows nor can change it. Postmodernism is an ideology insofar as it keeps us from changing the world for the better, something that is unlikely to happen in Las Vegas, the plastic surgeon's chair, or in front of the Jerry Springer show.

## BOURGEOISE AND PROLETARIAT

We need to examine one more aspect of Marx's materialist conception of history in order to understand its basic outlines. As the

---

**Bourgeoisie and Proletariat**

Engels defines these terms in a footnote to *The Communist Manifesto*: 'By bourgeoisie is meant the class of modern Capitalists, owners of the means of social production and employers of wage-labour. By proletariat, the class of modern wage-labourers who, having no means of production of their own, are reduced to selling their labour power in order to live' (*CM*: 219). The bourgeoisie, that is, are the owners of society's means of production of its material resources. The proletariat are the industrial labourers who have no resources but the wages they receive from the bourgeoisie. In *Capital*, Marx writes that modern society comprised three major classes: bourgeoisie, proletariat, and landowners. Nevertheless, he thinks of capitalism fundamentally as a mode of production that increasingly divides society into *two* economically antagonistic classes, the bourgeoisie and the proletariat. This antagonism will eventually reach such a crisis point, he argues, that the vast majority, the proletariat, will seize the means of production for themselves, and thereby for the whole of society.

forces of production develop in any given society – as new instruments of production are invented, new materials are discovered, new products become the material for more sophisticated products, means of distribution and exchange, and so on – they come to a point where they can no longer sustain the existing relations of production. After a series of crises, this economic contradiction reaches a point at which it is expressed as a social revolution, and the entire mode of production – along with all the political and cultural practices that derive from it – is altered. Western history, Marx and Engels argue, is the history of the development of this kind of economic crisis and social revolution. In *The Communist Manifesto*, Marx and Engels trace a coming revolution in contemporary capitalist society. The bourgeoisie, they argue, the middle-class owners of the means of production and distribution, who are the economically dominant class in the industrial capitalist mode of production, have been in power (by 1848) for little more than a hundred years. In that time, they have 'created more massive and more colossal productive forces than have all preceding generations together' (*CM*: 225). The invention of productive machinery on an ever-increasing scale; the scientific advances in industry, agriculture and engineering; the development of steam ships, canals, railways, the telegraph; the subjection and cultivation of vast areas of the globe; as well as the gathering of large bodies of the population into the cities for work, and the political centralization that follows from this – all these forces of production have been called into being by the bourgeoisie in order to further and maintain their economic dominance. Above all, Marx and Engels argue, the bourgeoisie has called into existence in vast masses, collected together in the industrial cities of the world, the *proletariat*, the army of industrial labourers who own nothing but the wages they receive for their labour. The proletariat own none of the commodities they produce, except what food and shelter they can buy in order to sustain themselves as labourers. Competition between individual capitalists for profit, and between individual labourers for work, drives their wages down to the minimum level at which they can be sustained as a class, and their working hours up to the maximum level.

Furthermore, as a result of the increasing division of labour, the work of the proletarian loses all individual character and pleasure for him. As Marx and Engels write, 'He becomes an appendage of the machine, and it is only the most simple, most monotonous, and most easily required knack that is required of him.' (*CM*: 227) Not only, therefore, are the lives of the vast majority of society under industrial capitalism reduced to an inhuman level of subsistence, Marx and Engels comment, but not even this subsistence can be guaranteed them, because of the constant crises of overproduction and unemployment caused by the fluctuations of the market. As Marx and Engels write, the bourgeoisie is 'incompetent to assure an existence to its slave within his slavery' (*CM*: 233). The combination of the increasing forces of production the bourgeoisie has brought into being, they argue, with the increasing misery of the proletariat on which they depend, can only result in the proletariat refusing any longer to be enslaved and to die for the bourgeoisie, and, assisted by communist intellectuals who understand the process of history, seizing the means of production for themselves. Marx and Engels write:

> The advance of industry, whose involuntary promoter is the bourgeoisie, replaces the isolation of the labourers, due to competition, by their revolutionary combination, due to association. The development of Modern Industry, therefore, cuts from under its feet the very foundation on which the bourgeoisie produces and appropriates products. What the bourgeoisie, therefore, produces above all, is its own grave-diggers. Its fall and the victory of the proletariat are equally inevitable.
>
> (*CM*: 233)

## MARX'S EARLY HUMANISM

As we will see in Chapter 2, Althusser's interpretation of Marx developed in opposition to the rise in post-war French philosophy of a humanist interpretation of Marx. Catholic philosophers Jean-Yves Calvez and Pierre Bigo, personalist philosophers Emmanuel Mounier and Althusser's former teacher Jean Lacroix, the existentialist Jean-

Paul Sartre and the phenomenologist Maurice Merleau-Ponty – to name only the most well known – had begun to incorporate Marxism into their own philosophies, on the grounds that, like their philosophies, Marx's work was concerned with the quality of human life. Marxism, these philosophers believed, is a system of thought concerned with liberating men and women from the inhuman conditions of capitalism and bringing about a society in which they are able to live genuinely human lives. As we will see, Althusser denies this. This kind of humanism, he argues, is a cunning ruse of capitalist ideology, duping well-meaning intellectuals into co-operation with precisely the kind of capitalism they are aiming to criticize. It has nothing whatever to do with Marxism. This was and continues to be a controversial view. The first thing Althusser has to do in order to argue it is to deal with the undeniable fact that, in his early work, Marx was quite explicitly a humanist.

The materialist conception of history was a system at which Marx arrived in 1845, with the *Theses on Feuerbach* and *The German Ideology*. In the 1844 manuscripts, unpublished until 1932, which have become known as the *Economic and Philosophical Manuscripts*, Marx's communist critique of capitalism was expressed in humanist language, which was not yet the language of the materialist concep-

---

**Humanism**

Marx's humanism does not consist in the emphasis on classical scholarship and eloquence characteristic of Renaissance humanism. Rather it is the kind of humanism developed in France and Germany in the eighteenth-century Enlightenment – the belief that men and women do in fact and should in principle govern their own lives. Althusser describes humanism as the theory of 'man at the centre of his world' (*ESC*: 198). The lives of men and women, in the humanist account, should be ordered at both the individual and the social levels by the principles of autonomous human reason. Inasmuch as he thinks of capitalism as a system that prevents people from determining their own lives in this way, and of communism as the means by which they can do so, the young Marx is a humanist.

tion of history. It was largely the increased attention paid to these manuscripts in post-war France that resulted in the many humanist interpretations of Marx to which Althusser objected. Philosophers who incorporated Marx's thought into their own argued that the kind of humanism explicit in the early work continued to constitute the implicit basis of his entire work. We will look at Althusser's critique of this view in the next chapter. In order to understand this critique, we will first look at Marx's early humanism, as expressed in the *Economic and Philosophical Manuscripts*.

The fundamental economic fact of capitalist production, Marx writes in the *Manuscripts*, is 'alienated labour'. By this he means several things. Firstly, the industrial labourer produces an object that he himself does not own, receiving in turn wages so low that he can buy for himself almost none of the objects so produced. Even today, you may make mass-produced children's toys in an Asian factory, but you will not be able to afford them for your own children. Since the production of commodities for sale is the economic basis of the industrial capitalist's power, then the more objects the labourer produces, the more he contributes to the power of the capitalist over him. The more he contributes to the global capitalist economy, the more the Asian worker contributes to precisely the economy that disadvantages him. This is what Marx means when he says that the product of the worker's labour confronts him as an 'alien' object, – one that, although he himself has produced it, stands over against him as an independent power. It is not only the product of labour that is alienated from the labourer by industrial capitalism, moreover. The worker is also alienated from himself. The division of labour, on which industrial capitalism depends, means that the industrial worker is not happy at work, since he is obliged merely to repeat at length a series of monotonous tasks. Ideally, for Marx, human labour is a process in which men and women transform both themselves and the natural world through their productive interaction with the latter. Labour for the industrial capitalist, however, develops neither the mental nor the physical capacities of the worker, but rather ruins both his mind and body. Furthermore, since, in Marx's view, it is the fundamental characteristic of human beings freely and consciously to produce their lives through their interaction with the natural world, the industrial labourer, who is unable to do this at work, is also alienated from his humanity. He can produce only what the capitalist requires him to produce, and this production does not further his life, but on the contrary diminishes it. Finally, Marx argues, industrial capitalism alienates the worker from his fellow man. The product of his labour stands over against him as an alien power precisely because it belongs to another person, the capitalist. As the worker diminishes his own life in producing this object, so he enriches the life of the capitalist, to whom it belongs.

This analysis of capitalism is not conducted in the social categories of the materialist conception of history, such as production relations and class struggle. Rather, for the Marx of the *Economic and Philosophical Manuscripts* the fundamental fact of capitalism is the alienation of the worker from all that should belong to him as a human being. He conceives of communism as the solution to this situation:

> Communism [is] the positive transcendence of private property as human self-estrangement, and therefore [is] the real appropriation of the human essence by and for man; communism therefore [is] the complete return of man to himself as a social (i.e., human) being – a return become conscious, and accomplished within the entire wealth of previous development.
>
> (*EPM*: 135)

If, under capitalism, the worker is alienated from that which is proper to him or her as a human being, as a result of the institution of private property on which capitalist production depends, then, under communism, as a result of the abolition of that institution, men and women will take these human characteristics back again. Communism is thus about becoming fully human again in a way that capitalism has made impossible. As serious attention began to be paid to the *Manuscripts* after World War II, philosophers and intellectuals found this account of communism persuasive. Althusser, however, would deny that it was an authentically Marxist account at all, despite the fact that Marx himself had written it. The young Marx, as he would put it, had not yet become Marx.

## SUMMARY

Marx and Engels develop a systematic philosophy they call the 'materialist conception of history'. According to this conception, a given society consists fundamentally of the forces and relations of production of its members' material lives. Out of this economic 'base' arises a 'superstructure', consisting of that society's legal and political institutions, and of all society's forms of consciousness, or 'ideology', including iyd literary and cultural production. Since human history has always been the history of class struggles, ideology is a discourse of class interest, reflecting the positions of the antagonistic classes in society, especially that of the ruling class. The kind of literary and cultural criticism that follows from the materialist conception of history, such as Althusser's, interprets the meaning of a given work in society by tracing the complex network of forces that have produced it as such. Marx arrived at this materialist conception of history after an intellectual journey through the humanism that characterizes his early work, in which he describes the alienation of men and women from their humanity under capitalism, and their re-appropriation of this humanity under communism.

# 2

# THE REVOLUTION IN THEORY: ALTHUSSER'S MARXISM

Althusser believed that Marx had effected a massive revolution in social science and philosophy, but that this revolution had been largely misunderstood, even by Marxists. Hence, his first major works consisted in a 'return to Marx', an attempt correctly to expound the immense significance of Marx's thought in theoretical discourses, from economics to literary criticism. Only by correctly understanding this revolution in theory, in Althusser's view, could Marxists effect the revolution in practice which was the purpose of all Marx wrote. In this chapter, we will look at Althusser's distinctive account of the radically new science of history that Marx founded. We will discuss the context in which Althusser developed this account, its fundamental elements, and its significance for literary and cultural criticism.

## MARXIST HUMANISM

Althusser first came to the attention of the French and international intellectual worlds with the publication in 1965 of two collections of papers. The first, *For Marx*, was a collection of essays he had been publishing mainly in Communist intellectual journals over the previous five years. The second, *Reading Capital*, was a series of papers read by

Althusser and a group of his Communist philosophy students at a seminar on Marx's *Capital* they had organized at the École normale supérieure in 1964–65. These two books immediately attracted widespread attention and controversy on the French intellectual scene, and quickly became influential texts in British and American literary studies, as an *avant-garde* of English-speaking critics began to work through the logic of the radical French philosophies of the 1960s in their own discipline.

We will begin by looking at the some of the contexts of these books. The first and most important context in which Althusser intended them as politically progressive interventions was that of *Marxist humanism*. Two facts above all had led to the massive rise to intellectual prominence of Communism in France after World War II. At the political level, the distinguished role played by the Communist Party in organizing the French Resistance to the Nazi occupation during the war had led many to see Communism as the only authentic means of political organization after the nightmare of the Third Reich. In 1946 membership of the French Communist Party was at a record 800,000. At the theoretical level, the publication of Marx's *Economic and Philosophical Manuscripts* in 1932, and their partial translation into French in 1937, led to the great influence of Marx's early humanist position, expressed in these manuscripts, in interpretations of Marxism as a whole. Suddenly, the technical formulas of *Capital* and the dry economic orthodoxies of the Communist parties became suffused with human significance, as Marx was newly read as a humanist philosopher. Understood in the light of his beliefs that capitalism was an inhuman system and that communism was the only kind of society in which people could live truly human lives, Marx began to be taken seriously by Catholics, personalists, existentialists, phenomenologists – in short, by philosophers and intellectuals of all kinds – and they began to write lengthy studies of his work and to incorporate it into their own. It was a period in which the celebrity existentialist philosopher Jean-Paul Sartre (himself newly converted to the cause of the proletariat) was able to describe Marxism as 'the untranscendable horizon of our time'. Even if not a card-carrying member of the Communist Party, an intellectual could not but take Marxism seriously.

During the effective dictatorship of the Soviet Union by Josef Stalin (1879–1953), the Communist parties of Europe were fiercely loyal to the USSR and to its leader. The role of Communist intellectuals, in France as elsewhere, was largely restricted during Stalin's reign to expounding the principles of Marxism so as to demonstrate the advantages of Soviet society over capitalist society. Stalin himself – depressingly described in this context by the faithful as the 'world's greatest philosopher' – had written a short book on Marxist philosophy, *Dialectical and Historical Materialism* (1938). For Stalin, Marxism was a complete and closed scientific system, called 'dialectical materialism', the truth of which Communist intellectuals were restricted to illustrating. Althusser describes the Stalin years, during which his career as a Communist philosopher began, as the 'dogmatist night' (*FM*: 31). During these years, the influence of Marxist humanism in philosophy outside the Communist Party was largely ignored as just one more form of capitalist denigration of the truth of Marxism. All that changed, however, in 1956, when Communist philosophers also jumped onto the humanist bandwagon.

In February 1956, Nikita Khrushchev, First Secretary of the Communist Party of the Soviet Union (CPSU), delivered his famous 'secret speech' at the Twentieth Congress of the CPSU. Summoning the delegates back from their hotels rooms after the Congress had apparently finished, Khrushchev denounced, with detailed facts and figures, the massive crimes against the Soviet people that Stalin had committed while in power. These crimes are of course no secret today, nor were they unknown to non-Communist observers of the Soviet Union at the time, but to the hundreds of thousands of ordinary members of Communist parties throughout the world, they came as a revelation. Talk of Stalinist repression by Western intellectuals and politicians had always been dismissed as capitalist slander. Suddenly, the International Communist movement was informed that it had all been true. Khrushchev initiated a programme of 'de-Stalinization', in which the errors and crimes of Stalin were denounced and corrected in order that (in theory, at least) they should not occur again. This is not the place to discuss the obviously self-serving motivation of Khrushchev's programme. The point for us is that this is where the Communist philosophers come in. Stalin's errors were held in part to be doctrinal. The door thus became open for Communist intellectuals to rethink Marxist doctrine for the first time in three decades. Reacting as enthusiastically as their non-Communist counterparts had to the new light thrown on Marx's thought by the *Economic and Philosophical Manuscripts*, Communist intellectuals shed with relief the Stalinist orthodoxies previously imposed upon them, and began to rethink Marxism in terms of the humanism of the *Manuscripts*. In the years following World War II, as a result, it was widely agreed by French intellectuals that Marxism was a system that aimed to end the capitalist alienation of the worker from his humanity by promoting the fully human life only possible in a Communist society. As Mark Poster writes in his book on French philosophy of the period:

> Almost unanimously, the commentators on the *1844 Manuscripts*, from the Communist Lefebvre to the Catholic Calvez, took the position that there was but one Marx and that the concept of alienation in the *1844 Manuscripts* was the fulcrum of all Marx's thought.
>
> (Poster 1975: 69)

Even the CPSU started talking the language of humanism. In 1961, at the Party's Twenty-Second Congress, Khrushchev described the new Party programme as 'a document of true Communist humanism', and as 'a full realization in practice of the Party slogan, "Everything for the sake of man, for the benefit of man"' (CPSU 1961: 189–90). It was this Marxist humanism, massively prevalent on the French intellectual scene by 1960, that Althusser first set out to criticize.

## STRUCTURALISM

The most prominent development on the French intellectual scene when Althusser wrote the essays in *For Marx* and *Reading Capital* was the radical new methodology in the social sciences known as *structuralism*. Structural linguistics had been founded by the Swiss linguist Ferdinand de Saussure (1857–1913) with the posthumous publication of his *Course in General Linguistics*, given in Geneva in 1911. Whereas the European philological tradition had been concerned with the historical development and comparison of languages, Saussure argued that linguistics could only achieve scientific status if it took as the object of its study the structure of a given language. Linguistics was not about the historical facts of actual speech (in Saussure's French, *parole*) but the structure at a single historical moment of a given language (or *langue*). The units of language, so conceived, Saussure called 'signs', which could be conceptually divided into two parts, the 'signifier' and the 'signified'. Signifiers are the *sound-patterns* of a language, comprising single units of recognizable sound. Signifieds are the *concepts* associated with those sound-patterns by the language's speakers. Saussure argued that linguistic signs are not meaningful in themselves, but are recognizable as such only by virtue of their *difference* from all the other signs in the system. Every unit of language, from the smallest sound-pattern up, is meaningful only in terms of its relationship to all the other comparable units in that language. Sound-patterns, vocabulary, word-formations, syntactical rules, meanings, and all other elements of language, Saussure claimed, function in a comparable way to the colours in a traffic light. A red light has no meaning in itself. But in the system of traffic rules, by virtue of its difference from the other elements in the system – 'amber light' and 'green light' – it acquires the meaning 'stop'. All of language works on this principle, Saussure argued – it consists of systems of units whose meaning derives only from their difference from the other units in the system.

Saussure argued that linguistics should constitute part of a larger science he called *semiology*, or the study of signs (from the Greek *semeion*, 'sign'). Social life involves all kinds of systems of signs, of which language was, by the time of the *Course in General Linguistics*, the only one to have been the object of scientific enquiry. Structuralism consisted in a response, across the human sciences – from anthropology to psychoanalysis to literary criticism – to Saussure's call to develop the principles of a general semiology. The anthropologist Claude Lévi-Strauss (b. 1908) argued that anthropological phenomena, such as myths, kinship systems, religious rites and the like, could be understood in the same way that Saussure had understood linguistic phenomena, as systems of units each of whose significance derives from their relationship to the other units in the system. From the late 1950s, literary critics in France began to develop structuralist methods. As with Lévi-Strauss, their goal was a truly scientific understanding of literary texts, through a knowledge of the deep structures from which such texts were generated. An early work of criticism that influenced many structuralists was the analysis of Russian fairytales by the Russian philologist Vladimir Propp (1895–1970). Beneath the multiplicity of characters and plot-events in the corpus of these tales, Propp discerned a finite number of 'spheres of action' and 'functions', of which every single tale was a combination of permutations. 'Spheres of action' underlie what appear as the characters in fairytales; Propp discerned seven of these, such as 'villain', 'helper', and 'hero'. 'Functions' underlie what appear as events in the plot; Propp discerned thirty-one of these, such as 'One of the members of a family absents himself from home', or 'An interdiction is addressed to the hero'. All the fairytales in the Russian corpus consisted of a combination of some of the seven spheres of action with some of the thirty-one functions. Every one of the tales, Propp concluded, was generated from a single structure of units and rules of combination. French structuralist criticism in the 1960s refined this basic principle. The linguist A.J. Greimas (1917–1992) argued that all narratives derive from a complex combinatory scheme of differential units of narrative meaning, which he classified in detail. The Bulgarian literary critic Tzvetan Todorov (b. 1939) analysed Giovanni Boccaccio's medieval collection of tales, the *Decameron*, as a series of articulations of a 'grammar' of narrative units and rules of combination, closely analogous to the grammatical units and rules of combination of language that generate sentences. The most brilliant of the structuralist literary critics was Roland Barthes (1915–1980), who analysed cultural phenomena from fashion to wrestling matches to striptease as systems of cultural signification. Before he developed a 'post-structuralist' position in about 1970, Barthes worked out an increasingly detailed methodology for the structural study of literary narratives as patterns of combination of differentially significant units.

By the mid-1960s, structuralism was the height of fashion in French intellectual life. Althusser was not a card-carrying structuralist, nor even a 'structuralist Marxist', as some introductory books on literary theory call him even today. Rather, he wrote his seminal papers in *For Marx* and *Reading Capital* in an intellectual *milieu* in which structuralism, as the dominant methodology, provided him with certain approaches to the interpretation of Marx's work. There are two such aspects to structuralism's influence on Althusser's Marxism. In the first place, structuralism was *anti-humanist*. Structuralists denied that cultural phenomena were the product of conscious decisions of individual human beings. Rather, they were the products of abstract social codes, of which individuals made use as members of the society governed by those codes. A literary text, from the structuralist point of view, was the product of a trans-individual *system* of literary meaning, rather than the creation of an individual author. Althusser would argue that, in Marxism properly understood, society itself is a system of relationships – each of whose elements can be understood only in terms of its relation to all the other elements in the system. So a society's literary products (let us say, the Victorian novel) can only be understood in terms of their relationship to all the other kinds of social activity that comprised the society that produced them – Victorian society's economy, political life, legal system, education system, marriage and family practices, colonial practices, religious institutions, publishing industry, and so on. Secondly, following from this anti-humanism, Althusser understands a society as a system of *elements in relationship*. He differs from classical structuralism, which tended towards a complete taxonomy of all the elements in a given system, and towards a 'grammar', or system of rules of combination, of these elements. Althusser is interested only in correctly understanding Marx, and correctly acting upon this understanding. Nevertheless, his account of Marx's revolutionary new theory of society shares with structuralist accounts of cultural phenomena the property of being a system of individual elements, each of whose significance consists in its relationship to the others in the system.

## PROBLEMATICS

Having established the context in which Althusser wrote, we will now go on in this chapter to see what his anti-humanist, pro-structuralist account of Marxism looks like. In the first place, it involves establishing exactly what Marxism is. This is not merely of theoretical interest to Althusser; it is politically important to understand Marx's thought correctly, he believes, because only if it is understood correctly can Marxists *act* on it successfully, and bring about the kind of just society that is the goal of Communist practice. He often cites the maxim of the Russian revolutionary V.I. Lenin (1870–1924): 'Without revolutionary theory, no revolutionary practice', and indeed this could function as the motto for Althusser's entire work. In order to understand Marx's revolutionary thought, Althusser argues, it is first of all crucial to understand what it is *not*. First on this list is the early work of Marx himself. It is a mistake, in Althusser's view, to incorporate the humanism of the young Marx into the theory that Marx began to develop in 1845. Although all the contemporary interest in Marx was based on precisely the opposite assumption, Althusser denies that 'we [risk] losing the *whole of Marx*' if we submit the work of his youth to a historical critique in the light of his later thought. On the contrary, Marxist theory *necessitates* such a critique. If Marx's early work is to be properly understood, Althusser argues, then it is necessary to read it in the light of a truly Marxist theory of ideology. Now, all the contemporary studies on the work of the young Marx – one of Althusser's earliest essays in *For Marx* is a review of a volume of several such studies – understandably *compare* Marx's early work (especially the *Manuscripts*) with his later work (especially *Capital*). One element of the *Manuscripts* is said to belong to thinkers who influenced Marx at the time, such as Hegel or Feuerbach; another is said to belong authentically to Marx's thought because it is recognizable in his later work. Althusser rejects this kind of comparative analysis. The Marxist theory of ideology, he argues, is based on quite different principles than those at work in such discussions. The first is this:

> Every ideology must be regarded as a real whole, internally unified by its own *problematic*, so that it is impossible to extract one element without altering its meaning.
>
> (*FM*: 62)

This is the first principle of Althusser's interpretation of Marx: that an individual system of thought has an internal unity that governs and determines all that is thought within it. This internal unity he calls its 'problematic', which he defines as 'the constitutive unity of the effective thoughts that make up the domain of the existing *ideological field*' within which an author thinks (*FM*: 66). He means that every philosophy is structured as such by a set of concepts that governs not only the solutions an author gives to the problems she poses, but also the problems themselves that can be posed. The problematic within which an author thinks, whether a novelist or a philosopher, is the system of concepts which governs the questions she can ask, and therefore the answers that can be given to them. Hence Althusser describes it as 'the system of *questions* commanding the *answers*' given by an individual author (*FM*: 67).

We can see the formulation of a new problematic at work in structuralism, for example. When Saussure defined a language as a system of signs, each comprising a signifier and a signified, and each of which had meaning only in terms of its difference from the other signs in the system, he opened up a new system of thought within which questions about language could be posed and answered. The European philological tradition from which he broke in founding structural linguistics was able to see the historical development of elements in languages from more ancient to more recent forms, and to compare elements of one language with elements of another. The system of methodological concepts available to it did not allow the structure of a single language at a given point in history to appear, far less to be analysed. Saussure's problematic of sign, signifier and signified caused a whole system of relationships to become visible to the science of linguistics that had previously remained unseen. In the same way, when the American linguist Noam Chomsky (b. 1928) broke with American structural linguistics to found the problematic of generative grammar, another new set of terms – deep structure, surface structure, universal grammar, language acquisition device, and the like – brought linguistic phenomena to the attention of scientific inquiry that simply had not figured on the radar screen of structural linguistics. Althusser thought of the concept of the problematic only with reference to philosophy, but it is possible to use it in literary analysis too. So it might be argued, for example, that Sylvia Plath, who died in 1963, just as the women's movement was beginning in America and Britain, was unable to make use of the terms of a feminist problematic, but was clearly searching for such terms in her work. Some of the violence of her later poetry is that of thoughts and feelings looking for expression, but since these thoughts and feelings are necessarily couched in a pre-feminist conceptual system, they can find expression only in the violent content and imagery that make the poetry so striking.

Althusser argues that this concept of the problematic, although not explicitly formulated by Marx, is nevertheless at work in his theory of ideology: 'Marx never directly used it, but it constantly animates the ideological analyses of his maturity (particularly *The German Ideology*)' (*FM*: 66). He gives the following citation from *The German Ideology* as an example:

> German criticism ... by no means examines its general philosophic premises, but in fact all its problems originate in a definite philosophical system, that of Hegel. Not only in its answers but even in its questions there was a mystification.
>
> (*GI*: 34)

Althusser points out that, when Marx's early work is analysed in terms of its problematic, the conclusion must be drawn that this work is not Marxist. Contemporary analyses of the young Marx had divided his work into elements that were recognizably Marxist and elements taken from previous philosophers, such as Feuerbach, whose influence Marx acknowledges in the *Manuscripts*. But when the Marxist concept of the problematic is understood, Althusser writes, then 'everything depends on a question which has priority over [these elements]: the question of *the nature of the problematic which is the starting-point for actually thinking them*, in a given text' (*FM*: 68). The problematic of Marx's early work, Althusser argues, is clearly the humanistic problematic of Feuerbach's philosophy, rather than the authentically Marxist problematic of the materialist conception of history, recognizable in Marx's work from 1845 onwards. No matter how little Marx explicitly refers to Feuerbach in his early work, and no matter how much he analyses objects which the latter does not, Althusser argues, the system of concepts within which he undertakes these analyses is that of Feuerbach, and not the one Marx himself developed in 1845, the materialist conception of history.

## THE 'EPISTEMOLOGICAL BREAK'

In 1845, Althusser argues, Marx's thought undergoes a complete and radical change. In the *Theses on Feuerbach* and *The German Ideology*, Marx abandons the entire problematic of humanism within which he had thought until then, and formulates an entirely new set of concepts with which to analyse society and its history. Althusser describes this event as follows:

> In 1845, Marx broke radically with every theory that based history and politics on an essence of man. This unique rupture contained three indissociable elements.
> 1  The formation of a theory of history and politics based on radically new concepts: the concepts of social formation, productive forces, relations of production, superstructure, ideologies, determination in the last instance by the economy, specific determination of the other levels, etc.
> 2  A radical critique of the theoretical pretensions of every philosophical humanism.
> 3  The definition of humanism as an ideology.
>
> (*FM*: 227)

In 1845, that is, Marx rejected the humanist problematic within which he had worked until then and established the terms of a new problematic, that of the materialist conception of history. Althusser understands the materialist conception of history as a *science*, that is, as a system of concepts which produces true knowledge of the history of societies. It is only by breaking with the problematic of humanism, and with all the philosophical concepts implicit in it, Althusser argues, that Marx founds the science of history. He writes: 'This rupture with every philosophical anthropology or humanism is no secondary detail; it is Marx's scientific discovery' (*FM*: 227).

Althusser uses the orthodox Communist term 'historical materialism' to describe the materialist conception of history considered as the science of history. Borrowing a term from the French philosopher of science Gaston Bachelard (1884–1962), Althusser describes Marx's foundation of this science of historical materialism as an 'epistemological break'. In Bachelard's view, the history of science progresses by means of a constant series of ruptures, in which both 'common sense' and previous scientific theories are completely rejected and replaced with a new theoretical system. Epistemology is the theory of knowledge, and so Althusser describes this kind of rupture as an epistemological break because it represents a completely new form of knowledge, in this case of history. In fact, it was only with this epistemological break that history became open to truly scientific knowledge at all, he argues. The term also emphasizes that, when Marx broke with the problematic of humanism in order to establish the problematic of historical materialism, he broke with an ideology in order to found a science. We only thought we were doing history before Marx; it is only after Marx that historians are truly able to understand and represent historical events – previously they had been ideologically misunderstanding and misrepresenting them. It is a radical claim, and one that many historians – even Marxist historians like E. P. Thompson – dispute. Like

## DIALECTIC

The term 'dialectic', which derives from the Greek term for the art of debating, has a great variety of meanings in the history of philosophy. In Plato's earlier dialogues, it is the art of philosophical discussion, of searching for truth by the process of question and answer. In Hegel's philosophy of mind, the history of thought progresses by means of the continual development of a concept into its opposite, and then into a higher form that unifies these two opposites. Because this process is one of contradiction and resolution, like the Greek art of discussion, Hegel calls it dialectic. In Marx's view, with this concept of dialectic Hegel had discovered the laws of historical progression, but had wrongly applied them to the history of thought. In reality, for Marx, it is society that progresses dialectically. Capitalist society, for example, generates the proletariat, which will destroy that society and bring in a higher form of it, communism, in which its industrial products will be used for the common good. In his later work, Engels develops this view. In opposition to the philosophical presupposition that objects are stable, individual entities, dialectical thought, of which Marxism is the highest form, understands the interconnections between things, and the processes of change, conflict and contradiction by which they are continually developing. In Marxist theory, 'dialectical materialism' became the name for the general science of nature, history and thought thus conceived, and 'historical materialism' the name for Marx's specific application of this science to the history of society.

the concept of the problematic, Althusser argues, that of the epistemological break was not explicitly formulated by Marx, but it is nevertheless implicit in his work.

## THE SCIENCE OF HISTORY

Not only did Marx break with the problematic of humanism in order to found that of historical materialism, Althusser argues, but he also broke with the problematic of the idealist philosopher G.W.F. Hegel, with which both Marx himself and Marxist tradition have always associated Marx's thought. In the postface to the second edition of *Capital* (1873), Marx claims specifically to have retained the 'dialectical method' of analysis from Hegel. He writes:

> The mystification which the dialectic suffers in Hegel's hands by no means prevents him from being the first to present its general forms of motion in a comprehensive and conscious manner. With him it is standing on its head. It must be inverted, in order to discover the rational kernel within the mystical shell.
>
> (C: 103)

The dialectic is the method Hegel used in analysing the history of thought, which he conceived of as the most fundamental reality of human history. Broadly speaking, it presupposes that every state of affairs is constantly developing into its own opposite or 'negation' (in the way that life, for example, is constantly developing into its opposite, death). When Marx says that, in Hegel, this method is standing on its head, and that he had to invert it, he means two things. Firstly, that history progresses in a dialectical manner, as Hegel had claimed. Secondly, he means that history is not fundamentally the history of ideas, as Hegel believed, but rather the material history of human society. From Engels on, Marxists had always interpreted this passage from *Capital* to mean that Marxism was a system of thought that incorporated the dialectical method first formulated by Hegel. Althusser denies this. It follows from the Marxist concepts of the problematic and the epistemological break, he argues, that when Marx founded the science of historical materialism, he established an entirely new system of concepts, which bear no resemblance to those of the earlier ideological problematics from which he broke, including that of Hegel. The Marxist problematic, although it is a dialectical system of thought (that is, it understands states of affairs to be continually developing into their own negation), is nevertheless altogether different from Hegel's dialectical system of thought. It is in specifying this difference that Althusser begins to set out in positive terms the content of the Marxist problematic, and to give an explicit account of the concepts in whose terms Marx understands society, its history, and its literary and cultural production.

In the first place, Althusser argues, the problematic of historical materialism consists of an entirely new set of *terms*. Whereas earlier social and economic thought had understood society as the sum of its individual agents, each of which was considered as a subject – the origin of his or her own thoughts, desires and actions – Marx thought in terms of the *mode of production*. A society's mode of production, as we saw in chapter 1, is the 'deeper, more concrete reality' (*FM*: 110) that, in the Marxist view, determines all the thoughts, desires and actions of its members. Althusser writes:

> Thus for the first time individual economic behaviour ... is measured according to its *conditions of existence*. The degree of development of the *forces of production*, the state of the *relations of production*: these are from now on the basic Marxist concepts.
>
> (*FM*: 110)

In the same way, Marx entirely transformed the political concept of the state, by considering it for the first time in relation to the concept of *social class*. Hence, although he retains the term 'state' from earlier political thought, Marx gives it an entirely new meaning, as an institution at work in the interests of the ruling or exploiting class. Althusser writes:

> The intervention of this new concept and its interconnexion with one of the basic concepts of the economic structure transforms the *essence of the State* from top to toe, for the latter is no longer above human groups, but at the service of the ruling class.
>
> (*FM*: 110)

In the second place, Althusser argues, the Marxist problematic consists of new *relations between its terms*, in comparison to the system of relations at work in previous philosophies. As we know, Marx divides societies into their economic base and their superstructure (the political, legal and ideological forms that develop out of the base). Althusser analyses an important passage from Engels which indicates that, while ideology is a part of a society's superstructure, determined in form and content by its economic base, this determination is not a simple matter of cause and effect. The economic base, that is, is not the *only* factor that influences superstructural elements of a society, such as its ideologies. Rather, although the forces and relations of production are always the *finally* determining cause of the various elements of the superstructure, these elements also influence each other and even the economic base itself. In a letter of 1890, Engels writes:

> According to the materialist conception of history, the *ultimately* determining element in history is the production and reproduction of real life. More than this neither Marx nor I ever asserted. Hence if somebody twists this into saying that the economic element is the *only* determining one he transforms that proposition into a meaningless, abstract, senseless phrase. The economic situation is the basis, but the various elements of the superstructure – political forms of the class struggle and its results, to wit: constitutions established by the victorious class after a successful battle, etc., juridical forms, and even the reflexes of all these actual struggles in the brains of the participants, political, juristic, philosophical theories, religious views, and their further development into systems of dogmas – also exercise their influence upon the course of the historical struggles and in many instances preponderate in determining their *form*.
>
> (SC: 498)

Elements of a society's superstructure like literary works are determined in form and content by the economic base of that society only *in the last instance*. They are also determined by every other element of the superstructure – political and legal forms, philosophy, religion, science, the media, and so on – as well, in the case of literary works, by the literary and cultural traditions already available in a given society. Each of these determining elements is itself finally determined in nature by the economic base of the society that has produced it. This economic base, however, acts upon literary and cultural products not only directly, but also through the complex mediation of all the elements of a society's superstructure upon which it also acts. Furthermore, literary and cultural products themselves, according to this view, react back upon other superstructural elements such as philosophy or politics and even back upon the economic base itself. So the influence of each level of a society's production on the others is, although finally traceable to the economic level, in reality a complex and dialectical network of mutual determination.

Althusser takes Engels to be expounding Marx's mature thought in this passage. Marx thinks of the relationship between base and superstructure, Althusser writes, in an entirely new way. Hegel had thought of each of the various aspects of the life of a society as a kind of expression of a single principle or idea, which unified that society. Ancient Rome, for example, he saw as the expression of the abstract legal personality. For Marx, on the other hand, the different aspects of the life of a society, including its literary and cultural products, are not expressions of any fundamental truth about that society. Rather they are on the one hand determined in the last instance by the economic base of that society, not only directly but also through the mediation of the various levels of the superstructure. Each of these superstructural levels, on the other hand, although finally determined by the economy, also influences its own future development, all the other superstructural levels, and the economic base itself. Althusser calls this the 'relative autonomy' and the 'specific effectivity' of the superstructure. By 'relative autonomy' he means that a given level of the superstructure (such as literary production) has its own history, which is traceable back to that of the economy only through a complex series of mediations. By 'specific effectivity' he means that each level of the superstructure can and does affect the history and development of all the other levels, including that of the economy.

In the Marxist problematic, then, a society is a complex structure consisting of different levels of activity that influence one another in a complex set of mutual relationships. Now, Marx has not explicitly worked out the nature of these relationships. Althusser writes:

> These specific relations between [base] and superstructure still deserve theoretical elaboration and investigation. However, Marx has at least given us the 'two ends of the chain', and has told us to find out what goes on between them: on the one hand *determination in the last instance by the (economic) mode of production*; on the other *the relative autonomy of the superstructures and their specific effectivity*.
>
> (*FM*: 111)

Borrowing a term from psychoanalysis, Althusser argues that social phenomena, from political parties to literary texts, are, in the terms of the Marxist problematic, *overdetermined*. In psychoanalysis, objects are said to be overdetermined when they have more than one cause. So, for example, if one dream-image represents two or more of the dreamer's thoughts, it is described as overdetermined. Althusser argues that, in the Marxist problematic, every aspect of a society is overdetermined in an analogous way – that is, it is caused in varying degrees by events and actions in all the levels of the base and superstructure by which it is constituted. He describes this process as follows:

> [It] should be called the *accumulation of effective determinations* (deriving from the superstructures and from special national and international circumstances) *on the determination in the last instance by the economic*
>
> (*FM*: 113).

While any given fact in the life of a society, from a news report or a novel to a revolution, is always determined in the last instance by the economic base of the society in which it was produced, it is also always determined, in varying degrees, by all the other levels of that society. In fact, Althusser argues, there is never any instance in which the economy is the sole determinant factor of a given historical event. Although Marxists speak in theory of the economy being determinant in the last instance, he writes, in reality 'the "last instance" never comes' (*FM*: 113). The economy and all the levels of the superstructure are *always* influencing each other's development, that is, in every instance of the history of every society.

Let us return to my earlier literary example of Sylvia Plath. The significance of Althusser's theory of society for criticism of her work is this.

First, as a body of literary production, that work has a relative autonomy from the economic situation in which it was produced, with obvious precursors and influences at the purely literary level, such as the poetry of Robert Lowell, Theodore Roethke and Anne Sexton. Second, a whole range of social factors also influences her poetry – they make it the kind of work it is – each of which both influences all the others, and can all ultimately, but not simply, be traced back to the economic practices of the society in which they occur. So Plath's work is conditioned by 1950s gender ideology (which privileged marriage and family for women), an education system that provided her with a world-class university education, the politics of the Cold War, the American history of immigration (her parents were born in Germany and Austria), the employment patterns of immigrants, their cultural expectations (her mother's literary ambitions and culture of self-improvement), pension and life-insurance practices (important after her father's death), the publishing industry, cultural expectations about work and remuneration, the practices of raising children, the history of psychiatric treatment, divorce law, to name only a few of the social systems within which she lived and worked. On Althusser's account, each of these social systems (a) is relatively autonomous, with its own specific history; (b) influences, in varying degrees, each of the other systems, including the capitalist economy in which they all exist; (c) is influenced, in varying degrees, by all the other systems; (d) is conditioned ultimately by the economy. So, gender ideology in America in the 1950s, for example, most obviously influences the publishing industry, divorce law, child-rearing and psychiatry. It is in turn influenced by the history of World War II (in which American women entered the work force in great numbers, and to which the 1950s ideology of home was in part a reaction, once the economy was re-filled with demobbed servicemen) the mass production of household appliances, religious ideology and so on. Each of these social systems, through their complex pattern of mutual effect on one another, can ultimately be traced to the economy. The publishing industry and the production of consumer goods are obviously governed by economic concerns; psychiatry depends on technological developments and production, a university system and a hospital system, all of which need investments of capital, and particular patterns of income in order to be accessible. This is what

Althusser's theory of society means for literary and cultural criticism. A given cultural product is considered neither as the work of an individual genius (as in traditional bourgeois criticism) nor simply as a product of the economy (as in traditional Marxist criticism). Rather, it is considered as the complex product of what Althusser calls its *conjuncture*, the complex network of mutually influential social systems that comprise a society at any given historical moment. Literary criticism, in the light of this theory of society, can trace the ways in which these complex networks of influence have made a given work the particular work that it is.

Althusser specifies that each of the levels by which a society is constituted, as well as that society as a whole, is governed by 'the law of uneven development' (*FM*: 201). In the first place, that is, the relative influence of each of the social levels upon all the others is different at any given period; the political level, for example, may be the most strongly determining force on all the other levels, the economy the next most powerful, and so on. During the Cold War, with the development of nuclear weapons, technology arguably exercised a stronger influence on Western societies than even the economy, to which it was dialectically related. In the second place, the most influential of the social levels – Althusser calls it the 'dominant' level – changes as given societies develop. There is always a level that is more influential than all the others, Althusser argues. Which level this is, however, changes throughout history. A society always constitutes a 'structure in dominance', Althusser writes – that is, a structure of levels of activity that mutually influence one another's development, and in which one level is the most influential. This is what he means when he writes that 'the complex whole [of a society] has the unity of a structure articulated in dominance' (*FM*: 202). This means that the levels of literary and cultural production are influenced by a changing set of relations between all the other levels of the societies in which they are produced. The mass media and communications technology have become much more influential in postmodern cultural production, for example, than they were in the modernist period before World War II. Furthermore, each social level itself, such as the level of literary production, develops unevenly, determined as it is by a changing complex of influence from all the other levels. This dual unevenness – that of each level of social activity, and that of the relationship between each of the levels — is the most fundamental characteristic of the Marxist view of a society, Althusser argues. In the terms of the Marxist problematic, he claims, a society consists precisely of this uneven set of relationships between its levels.

## PRACTICE

There is one more aspect of the Marxist problematic that we need to mention in order to understand Althusser's account of the science of historical materialism. So far, we have spoken of the different 'levels' by which a society is constituted (the economic level, the political level, and so on). In the Marxist problematic, Althusser argues, each of these levels can be defined as a *practice*. So he speaks of 'social practice', by which he means the sum total of all the distinct forms of practice existing in a given society. Each of its 'levels' of activity is also a form of practice, so a society consists of economic practice, political practice, ideological practice (which includes the practice of literary production), and so on. Althusser defines the term as follows:

> By *practice* in general I shall mean any process of *transformation* of a determinate given raw material into a determinate *product*, a transformation effected by a determinate human labour, using determinate means (of 'production'). In any practice thus considered, the *determinant* moment (or element) is neither the raw material nor the product, but the practice in the narrow sense: the moment of the *labour of transformation* itself, which sets to work in a specific structure, men, means and a technical method of utilizing the means.
> 
> (*FM*: 166)

The essence of practice, in Althusser's account, is labour. It is a process in which a raw material is transformed into a finished product by men and women using a given set of skills, instruments and forms of organization. In economic practice, natural materials (such as cloth) are transformed into products (such as clothes) by the industrial labour of textile workers. In political practice, the raw materials of social relations are transformed into the product of new social relations by the work of political organizations and the policies on which they are based. Every level of activity by which a society is constituted in the Marxist problematic, Althusser argues, consists of a practice of this kind, with a specific set of raw materials, means of production and finished product. As we will see later, Althusserian literary critics have understood the practice of literary production in different ways, but for now we can note the following. Literary production, in Althusser's account of the Marxist problematic, works on the raw material of the ideological representations of people's lives that are at work in a given society; the set of ideological beliefs appropriated by a given author (her philosophical, religious, political convictions, and so on); and the events of her own history. Its means of production include the set of literary genres and forms of expression available to a given author, the forms of publication, distribution and consumption at work in the society in which she writes, and her imagination, which is determined by the social conditions in which it is exercised. Its finished product is the literary work.

## ALTHUSSERIAN LITERARY CRITICISM

An example of the kind of literary criticism that follows from Althusser's account of the Marxist science of society can be found in an early work by the Marxist critic Terry Eagleton, *Myths of Power: A Marxist Study of the Brontës* (1975). Eagleton draws on Althusser's concept of overdetermination as he situates the work of the Brontë sisters in the complex and mutually determining levels of practice within which it was produced. He begins with an account of the economic relations between the landed aristocracy and the industrial bourgeoisie of the West Riding of Yorkshire during the period in which the Brontës wrote. He then analyses the political history of the region, which he argues was 'exceptionally complex, and certainly not directly reducible to the expression of economic interests' (Eagleton 1988: 6). He goes on to locate the Brontës' own social situation within this economic and political context. The educated daughters of a petit-bourgeois (i.e. lower-middle-class) clergyman, the sisters were unable to found a school of their own for lack of capital and social influence, and became governesses, 'trapped in an educational machinery set up by the rich to exploit the sons and daughters of the "genteel" poor' (Eagleton 1988: 10). The way in which they understood this situation, Eagleton argues, was further overdetermined by the struggle at the wider level of cultural practice between the Romantic imagination and the material pragmatism of industrial society. He writes:

> The Brontës' situation is, I believe, overdetermined in precisely [Althusser's] sense. The major historical conflict which this book selects as its focus – that between landed and industrial capital – is sharpened and complicated for the Brontës by a host of subsidiary factors. They happened to live in a region which revealed the conflict between land and industry in a particularly stark form – starker, certainly, than in a purely agrarian or industrial area. The same part of the country ... witnessed working-class struggle at an extraordinary pitch of militancy. ... These pervasive social conflicts were then peculiarly intensified by the sisters' personal situation. They were, to begin with, placed at a painfully ambiguous point in the social structure, as the daughters of a clergyman with the inferior status of 'perpetual curate' who had thrust his way up from poverty. ... They were, moreover, socially insecure *women*, members of a cruelly oppressed group whose victimised condition reflected more widespread exploitation. And they were *educated* women, trapped in an almost intolerable deadlock between culture and economics – between imaginative aspiration and the cold truth of a society which could use them merely as 'higher' servants ... And as if all this were not enough, they were forced to endure in their childhood an especially brutal form of ideological oppression – Calvinism.
>
> (Eagleton 1988: 8)

In thus drawing on the concept of overdetermination, Eagleton begins to follow through the logic of Althusser's theory of society for literary criticism. He interprets the work of the Brontë sisters as a complex product of the mutually determining social practices within which it was produced. As he acknowledges in the preface to the second edition of the book (1988), the study has flaws. In particular, the theory Eagleton develops in the introduction to the book is not well integrated into its critical practice as a whole. He only begins the economic, political and ideological analyses necessary fully to work out the logic of Althusser's theory of society in literary criticism. Furthermore, he comes to recognize that there are levels of social practice which he did not adequately take into account, especially that of gender politics, which he later came to see as the dominant practice in the determination of the Brontës' work. Nevertheless, Eagleton's study, if it does not fully work through the demanding consequences of Althusser's Marxism for literary criticism, clearly begins to do so. According to the logic of the Marxist science of society, he interprets the literary works of the Brontë sisters as overdetermined products of the complex series of social practices within which they were produced.

## SUMMARY

In this chapter, I have discussed Althusser's interpretation of Marx, which he thought of as an authentic reconstruction of Marx's thought in the face of contemporary misrepresentations of this thought. Althusser argues that every system of thought is internally unified by its own 'problematic', or system of concepts. It is impossible to understand any one of these concepts in isolation from the problematic in which it was formulated. This means that Marx's early work is not entirely or even partly Marxist, but rather written from the perspective of a problematic entirely foreign to Marxism, that of humanism. In 1845, there is an 'epistemological break' in Marx's thought, in which he rejects the humanistic ideology of his early work, and founds the science of historical materialism. According to the principles of this science, Althusser argues, a society is a complex structured whole, consisting of different levels of 'practice', or labour, in which given raw materials are transformed by given means of production into a finished product. Although economic practice always determines all the others in the last instance, in reality everything that occurs at every level of social practice, from political revolutions to literary texts, is determined in varying degrees by all the other levels. Althusser describes this process of multiple and uneven determination as 'overdetermination'. According to this account of society, literary production is a practice that is overdetermined by the complex set of influences upon it of all the other practices of the society in which it occurs.

# 3

# THE POLITICS OF READING: ESSAYS ON INTERPRETATION

As we will see below, one of the means by which Althusser arrived at his interpretation of Marx was through a distinctive method of reading, whose principles he found in Marx himself. He called this method 'symptomatic reading', because it involved reading texts in a similar way to that in which psychoanalysts read the symptoms of their patients, namely for a meaning of which the patients – or the texts' authors, in Althusser's case – are unconscious. In this chapter, we will examine this reading method, which Althusser finds at work in Marx's *Capital*, and which he then applies back to Marx's own texts. Althusser's symptomatic readings of theoretical texts raise the question of how a literary text could or should be read symptomatically. In order to answer this question, we will turn to the work of Althusser's student Pierre Macherey (b. 1938), who set out to work through the consequences of Althusser's interpretation of Marx for literary criticism. Althusser had specified the science of historical materialism, which Marx had founded; Macherey set out to formulate the literary theory and the critical practice that followed from this science. In the second section of this chapter, therefore, we will examine the literary theory that Macherey derives from Althusser's work, in which he describes literature as a process of production of a text from the raw materials of ideology. We will go on to examine one of Macherey's symptomatic readings of a literary text. In the final section, we will discuss the second definition of philosophy that Althusser developed from 1967 onwards, the 'class struggle in theory', concluding with an analysis of the politics of literary criticism that follows from this definition.

## SYMPTOMATIC READING

In his early work, Althusser argues, Marx's thought depended on what he calls the 'religious myth of reading' (*RC*: 17), according to which the world is a kind of Holy Scripture, a text that speaks truly to us. To look at a thing, according to this theory of knowledge, is to 'read' its essence, and thus truly to know it. Marx read the alienation of the human essence in capitalist production at sight – he only had to look around him, his work implies, to see the truth of human nature and its alienation. After the epistemological break, however, Althusser finds a 'new practice of reading' in his work, based on a 'theory of history capable of providing us with a new theory of reading' (*RC*: 18). This new theory and practice are found above all in *Capital*. As Althusser points out, Marx constantly quotes, often at length, from the work of previous economists in *Capital*. At first sight, he does this for the obvious purpose of criticizing what is false in what his predecessors have written and supporting his own claims by what is true in what they have written. On closer examination, however, Althusser argues, Marx's reading practice is more complex than this. To be precise, he argues, it is a 'double reading', or rather 'a reading which involves two radically different reading principles' (*RC*: 18). The first of these principles is a simple one. In the first kind of reading, Althusser argues, 'Marx reads his predecessor's discourse ... through his own discourse' (*RC*: 18). Marx reads the work of previous economists – that of Adam Smith (1723–1790), for example – in the light of the results of his own work. So he points out what Smith has discovered in the field of economics, and he points out what Smith has failed to see. There is a theory of knowledge implied in this kind of reading, Althusser argues, a theory in which knowledge is thought of ultimately as a kind of vision. Smith, according to Marx, has seen some economic facts and not seen others – the absence of these facts in his work represents an 'oversight'. The logic of this reading Althusser describes as follows:

> The logic of a conception of knowledge in which all the work of knowledge is reduced in principle to the recognition of the mere relation of *vision*; in which the whole nature of its object is reduced to the mere condition of a *given*.
> (*RC*: 19)

In the first kind of reading that Marx practices in *Capital*, that is, Althusser sees a presupposition that the objects of economic analysis are simply given, are 'out there' in the world, so that an acute economist like Marx can see them, whereas a less acute one like Smith can fail to see them.

This is not the only principle of reading at work in *Capital*, however. Althusser writes, 'There is in Marx a *second quite different reading*, with nothing in common with the first' (*RC*: 19). As an example of this kind of reading, Althusser cites a passage from chapter 19 of *Capital*, on wages, in which Marx argues that, in their discussions of the value of labour (i.e. how a worker's wages are determined), the major economists of the previous two hundred years had failed to formulate the crucial concept of *labour-power*. For Marx, it is because the capitalist buys a worker's labour-power (that is, his capacity for working in this or that particular way) that he is able to produce surplus-value, or profit. A capitalist sells his product for more than he paid to produce it. How is this possible? In Marx's view, it is because of the special value of labour-power. Marx holds (a theory current in 1867, but which most economists no longer hold) that the value of a commodity is the amount that it cost to produce it. The daily value of a worker's labour-power, therefore, is the amount that it costs to produce him each day as a labourer – that is, to feed, clothe and house him, and so on. If a worker can produce this amount of value (that is, if he can produce commodities which cost this much) in six hours, but he works for 12 hours a day, then in the final six hours of his day he is producing pure profit for the capitalist. In the first six hours, his employer is simply getting back the value of the amount he laid out on his wages, but in the second six hours, he is getting something (the product of the worker's labour) for nothing. This is why capitalism is an exploitative system: it depends upon the capitalist not paying the worker for a portion of the work he does. It seems that the worker is paid for his day's labour, but in fact he is only paid for the part of the day's expenditure of labour-power that it costs to produce the amount of commodities equivalent to the amount it costs to maintain him as a worker. For the rest of the day, he expends his labour-power for free. So the distinction in economics between labour and labour-power is crucial. Without it, economists are able to say that, in capitalist production, a worker is paid for a day's labour, which is untrue. In reality, although the worker is required to expend his labour-power for a whole day, he is only paid for doing so for a part of that day

This is what Marx says about the confusion between the two concepts in previous economic studies:

> Classical political economy believed it had ascended from the accidental prices of labour to the real value of labour. It then determined this value by the value of the subsistence goods necessary for the maintenance and reproduction of the labourer. *It thus unwittingly changed terrain* by substituting for the value of labour, up to this point *the apparent object of its investigations*, the value of labour-power, a power which only exists in the personality of the labourer, and is as different from its function, labour, as a machine is from its performance. ... The result the analysis led to, therefore, was *not a resolution of the problem as it emerged at the beginning, but a complete change in the terms of that problem*.
> (Cited in *RC*: 20–21; cf. *C*: 678–79)

This is an example of what Althusser describes as the second kind of reading that Marx practices in *Capital*. Whereas in the first kind of reading, Marx criticized earlier economists for not seeing given economic facts, in this second kind of reading he criticizes them for not having understood what they have seen. In this case, Althusser writes:

> The oversight, then, is not to see what one sees; the oversight no longer concerns the object, but *the sight* itself. The oversight is an oversight that concerns *vision*: non-vision is therefore inside vision, it is a form of vision and hence has a necessary relationship with vision.
> (*RC*: 21)

It is clear from this second kind of reading, Althusser argues, that a different theory of knowledge is implied to that implied in the first kind of reading. Knowledge can no longer be considered as a form of vision, of given objects, because according to Marx the major economists have seen certain objects in the field of their analysis, but they have nevertheless failed to come to know them. Knowledge is a process, therefore, in which it is possible not to see what you are looking at.

How is this possible? Althusser analyses Marx's reading practice in detail here. The essence of Marx's reading of the classic texts of economics is this. The economists have produced a kind of correct answer – they have asked the question, 'what is the value of labour?', and have replied, 'the value of labour is that of the subsistence goods necessary for the maintenance and reproduction of labour'. What Marx has noticed, Althusser points our, is that this answer is '*the correct answer to a question that has just one failing; it was never posed*' (*RC*: 22). In fact, this question is a kind of answer to the question, 'what is the value of labour-*power?*' How has Marx noticed this? It is because the answer given by classical economics does not make sense. What does the phrase, 'the maintenance and reproduction of labour' mean? Nothing. It makes sense to speak about maintaining and reproducing a 'labourer', but not 'labour'. If we change the answer of classical economics to, 'the value of labour is that of the goods necessary for the maintenance and reproduction of the labourer', however, it still does not make sense. According to the economists' own terms, the value of a commodity is equal to the cost of producing it. The value of the commodity 'labour' cannot therefore be defined by the cost of maintaining and reproducing the commodity 'labourer'. It is not the labourer but his labour that is bought for wages. What Marx shows, therefore, is that there are 'blanks', or absences, in the texts of the earlier economists. The answer they have produced to their question, 'What is the value of labour?', insofar as it can be defended, is something like this:

> 'the value of labour ( ) is equal to the value of the subsistence goods necessary for the maintenance and reproduction of labour ( )'
>
> (*RC*: 22)

As Althusser stresses, Marx has not imposed these bracketed blanks on the text from outside. Rather, he has shown that the text itself points to its own silences here. There is nothing wrong with the question, 'What is the value of labour?' What Marx observes is that the economists' answer to that question, in the way that it fails to make sense in the form in which it is expressed, indicates that it needs to be supplemented by another term in order to make sense. When it is so supplemented, it becomes clear that it constitutes the answer to a question that the economists did not pose, namely, 'What is the value of labour-power?' This is what Marx means when he says that the economists, instead of resolving the problem they had set themselves, in fact changed its terms. Althusser writes:

> Marx can pose the unuttered *question*, simply by uttering the concept present in an unuttered form in the emptinesses in the *answer*, sufficiently present in this answer to produce and reveal these emptinesses as the emptinesses of a presence.
>
> (*RC*: 23)

This, then, is the second kind of reading that Marx practices in *Capital*, and which is the practice most characteristic of his later work. It is a practice in which he restores to a text which contains gaps or contradictions in its meaning the missing terms it needs in order genuinely to make sense.

Althusser describes this kind of reading as a 'symptomatic' reading. He has in mind the process whereby a psychoanalyst interprets the symptoms of the person she analyses as signs of unconscious mental processes. In psychoanalysis, even the unusual features of ordinary speech can be interpreted, like neurotic symptoms, as signs of unconscious thoughts. The classic example is the 'Freudian slip', an apparent verbal mistake that nevertheless truly expresses unconscious thoughts – such as the wedding speech in which the groom, instead of saying that he would like to 'specially thank' the bridesmaids, announces that he would like to 'spank' them. By describing Marx's second kind of reading practice as symptomatic, Althusser means that he has read the classic texts of economics in a similar way to that in which a psychoanalyst reads the discourse of her patient. Marx has paid attention to the disturbances in the sense of the texts, interpreting these disturbances as signs of the presence of another, unwritten text – of a different and more fundamental set of ideas than those which the economists had intended to express.

Althusser describes this kind of reading practice as follows:

> [It is] a reading which might well be called '*symptomatic*', insofar as it divulges the undivulged event in the text it reads, and in the same movement related it to *a different text*, present as a necessary absence in the first. Like his first reading, Marx's second reading presupposes the existence of *two texts*, and the measurement of the first against the second. But what distinguishes this new reading from the old one is the fact that in the new one the *second text* is articulated with the lapses in the first.
>
> (*RC*: 28)

In a symptomatic reading, that is, it is no longer a question simply of reading the text under analysis against the grid of the reader's own ideas. Rather, it is a question of bringing to light the set of ideas indicated by the gaps, contradictions and other logical flaws in the text, and then of reading the text against these ideas. In Althusser's psychoanalytic metaphor, a symptomatic reading reconstructs the unconscious thoughts of a text, and interprets it on the basis of these thoughts.

The results of a symptomatic reading differ according to the nature of the text being read. In the case of Marx's readings of the classic economic texts, Althusser argues, the flaws he points out in the logic of these texts are a result of the different problematics within which the economists on the one hand, and Marx on the other, think. Economics before Marx could not understand the concept of labour-power as Marx did – as that which allows the capitalist to produce a profit by not fully paying his labourers – because its authors thought within a different framework of concepts than those with which Marx analysed the capitalist mode of production. So, when the classic texts of economics point to the concept of labour-power in the gaps and contradictions in their discourse on labour, Althusser argues, what has is occured is this. The logic of the economists' discourse has led them to the concept of labour-power, but becasue this discourse is formulated in terms of an ideological problematic, it cannot define or discuss this concept as such. The concept of labour-power is a part of the problematic of historical materialism, and can only appear directly in a discourse formulated in terms of this prob-

KEY IDEAS   57

lematic. The major economists before Marx had worked out the existence of the phenomenon that Marxists call labour-power, but because they did not think within the Marxist problematic they were not able to conceptualize or even to name it. They were unconscious of it, in short, and it is this unconscious aspect of their discourse on labour that Marx has discovered in its gaps and flaws. Having shown the existence of this method of reading in Marx, Althusser goes on to apply it to Marx's own texts. The logic of this reading of Marx goes like this. Marx has founded the science of historical materialism, which has consequences for the way in which we read texts, namely that they can be read symptomatically. Therefore, in order to read Marx's own texts according to the scientific principles of Marxism, it is necessary to read them symptomatically. This is a circular argument, as Althusser is aware. His justification of it goes something like this. All interpretation is circular – we are always learning how to interpret texts from the texts themselves that we are interpreting. The specifically Marxist version of this 'hermeneutic circle' is that we learn the principles of Marxist science from Marx's texts, and, the more we learn about this science from these texts, the more we learn how to read them in order to understand the science that they contain (*FM* 38–39).

Just as what Althusser called 'the religious myth of reading' was based on an implicit theory of knowledge, so is the Marxist method of symptomatic reading. Whereas the former thought of knowledge as a kind of vision, the latter thinks of it as a kind of production. As we saw in chapter 2, according to Althusser's reading of Marx, every practice in a society is a process of production. Each practice produces a given product out of a set of raw materials, by means of a given set of means of production. This is true of the practices that produce knowledge – the sciences, both the natural sciences and the human sciences, including literary criticism and cultural studies. Knowledge is produced out of a set of raw materials – in Althusser's view, more or less simple concepts or interpretations of the world. Its means of production is the problematic within which the scientist thinks. The product is knowledge – in the case of literary criticism, knowledge of a given literary work. Marx was able to read the gaps and contradictions in the texts of economics, Althusser argues, because their authors had produced the knowledge of the concept of labour-power, but since they were writing within an ideological problematic they were unable to understand and discuss that concept as such. Althusser is able to read the flaws in Marx's texts because, while Marx founded a new problematic, the process of doing so was a long and difficult one. Initially, because he has to create it from nothing, Marx does not have the language in which to express the new system of concepts he has founded. Hence his scientific system of thought is formulated unevenly, through the multiplication of metaphors for what he is trying to say. Or Marx may only have been able to answer a question in another part of his work than that in which he was able to pose it for the first time. In both cases, wherever a text has produced knowledge of a given field of analysis but has not been able directly to express that knowledge, it is accessible, in Althusser's view, to a Marxist symptomatic reading.

## MACHEREY: TEXT AND IDEOLOGY

In *Reading Capital*, Althusser is concerned with reading theoretical texts. Nevertheless, he repeats throughout his work that the science of historical materialism has consequences for the practice of reading literary texts. For example, in his preface to the French translation of *Capital*, he writes:

> The specialists who work in the domains of the 'Human Sciences' and of the Social Sciences ... i.e. economists, historians, sociologists, social psychologists, psychologists, historians of art and literature, of religious and other ideologies – and even linguists and psychoanalysts, all these specialists ought to know that they cannot produce truly scientific knowledges in their specializations unless they recognize the indispensability of the theory Marx founded. For it is, in principle, the theory which 'opens up' to scientific knowledge the 'continent' in which they work.
>
> (*LP*: 72)

In *A Theory of Literary Production* (1966), Althusser's student Pierre Macherey set out to work out the consequences of Althusser's interpretation of Marx for literary theory and criticism. On the basis of Althusser's formulation of the Marxist science of historical materialism, Macherey set out to formulate a scientific theory of literature and to practice a scientific literary criticism.

In order to produce genuine knowledge of a literary work, Macherey argues, as opposed to an ideological misrepresentation of it, literary criticism must avoid the ideological fallacies by which it has so far been characterized. In particular, it must avoid the 'interpretive fallacy', according to which the function of criticism is to expound the meaning contained in and expressed by the work. For Macherey, literary works do not contain a single or unified meaning that could be expounded by the kind of criticism he calls 'interpretive', and this is what he means by describing it as an ideological fallacy. The belief that a literary work contains a coherent system of meaning, for Macherey, is closely related to the belief that it is the creation of an individual author. According to this belief, the author knows what she is going to say in advance, and expresses this intention in her work. But, as Marx has shown us, in a way that Althusser has specified, the process of forming and expressing ideas occurs within social history and is determined by it. The literary work cannot be considered the 'creation' of an individual mind, therefore, but is the product of a socially determined process of production. As a result of the nature of this process, Macherey argues, literary works do not simply contain the meaning their authors intended to express in them, as a nutshell contains a nut, but are in fact made up of many different and conflicting meanings. He writes:

> To step out of the circle of critical fallacies, we must propose a theoretical hypothesis: the work does not contain a meaning which it conceals by giving it its achieved form. The necessity of the work is founded on the multiplicity of its meanings; to explain the work is to recognize and *differentiate* the principle of this diversity. *The postulated unity of the work which, more or less explicitly, has always haunted the enterprise of criticism, must now be denounced*: the work is not *created* by an intention (objective or subjective); it is *produced* under determinate conditions.
>
> (Macherey 1978: 78)

As a result of the conditions of their production, for Macherey, literary works comprise a complex and conflicting set of relations between different meanings. They do not have a unity, nor are they whole or complete, as literary criticism has often assumed. Rather, they are 'incomplete' or 'insufficient', or, as Macherey puts it most precisely, 'decentred' (Macherey 1978: 79). The principles by which their elements are related cannot be found in them. The model of literary criticism that Macherey proposes, therefore, is one that does not 'interpret' the meaning of a text, but rather 'explains' what the work itself does not, namely the reasons for its composition by a series of conflicting meanings. He writes:

> What begs to be explained in the work is ... the presence of a relation, or an opposition, between elements of the exposition or the levels of composition, those disparities which point to a conflict of meaning. ... The book is not the extension of a meaning; it is generated from the incompatibility of several meanings, the strongest bond by which it is attached to reality in a tense and ever-renewed confrontation.
>
> (Macherey 1978: 79)

Why do the conditions of production of literary works result in the kind of incompleteness, disparity or 'decentred-ness' that Macherey sees in them? It is because they are made out of ideology. The raw materials out of which literary works are produced are ideological materials – systems of belief and value, popular opinion, and all kinds of contemporary discourse, as well as the literary forms, themes and devices available to an author at her point in literary history. Ideology is a discourse of class-interest, which means that it misrepresents the reality of social relations in societies made up of antagonistic classes. This is what Macherey means when he describes it as the language of 'illusion' – that it refers to imaginary rather than to real objects. Ideologies have an apparent coherence, Macherey argues – they seem to represent a more or less complete account of the world and how to live in it. But in fact they are incomplete, since their function is precisely to efface the reality of the exploitative relations upon which society is based. As Macherey writes, 'Like a planet revolving around an absent sun, an ideology is made of what it does not mention; it exists because there are things which must not be spoken of' (Macherey 1978: 132). Now, when such ideological materials are produced into a literary work, Macherey argues, they change in character, just as wool, for example, changes in character when it is produced into a coat. When we live inside the everyday language of ideology – when, without critical reflection upon these activities, we participate in everyday speech, assume popular opinions, read the newspapers, watch television, and so on – its limits are not immediately apparent. When this language is fixed into the aesthetic form of a literary work, however, ideology's unspoken limits – the social realities of which it cannot speak, of which it exists in order not to speak – become apparent. When ideologies are represented in the form of a literary work, their incompleteness is also represented. Macherey writes:

> Since it is built from the formless language of illusion, the book revolves around this myth [i.e. the ideology out of which it is made], but in the process of its formation the book takes a stand regarding this myth, exposing it. ... The book gives an implicit critique of its ideological content, if only because it resists being incorporated into the flow of ideology in order to give a *determinate representation* of it.
>
> (Macherey 1978: 64)

This is the reason for the disparate, conflicting and contradictory structure of literary works. A literary work is made up of a series of conflicting elements, which do not form a coherent or consistent unity, because the ideologies out of which it is made are themselves only coherent or consistent to a limited extent, and are contradicted by the historical realities of which they exist not to speak. The internal disunity of the work is the result of the misrepresentative and limited character of the ideology from which it is made. This is the basis for Macherey's model of literary criticism as 'explanation' of the conflicting elements of literary works. Literary criticism based on the science of historical materialism, he argues, will explain the gaps, flaws and contradictions in literary texts in terms of their conditions of production from the raw materials of contemporary ideologies. It will explain the reasons for which the work fails to be the coherent or consistent unity that ideological literary criticism believes that it is. It will constitute a symptomatic reading of literary texts. Macherey describes this kind of reading as follows:

We must show a sort of splitting within the work: this division is *its* unconscious, in so far as it possesses one – the unconscious which is history, the play of history beyond its edges, encroaching on those edges: this is why it is possible to trace the path which leads from the haunted work to that which haunts it. Once again, it is ... a question of revealing in the very gestures of expression that which it is not. Then, the reverse side of what is written will be history itself.

(Macherey 1978: 94)

## SYMPTOMATIC LITERARY CRITICISM

Macherey offers a series of symptomatic readings of literary texts in *A Theory of Literary Production*, the most detailed of which is his reading of Jules Verne's *The Mysterious Island* (1875). This novel is a particularly clear example of a work that displays the kind of internal conflict that, Macherey argues, characterizes every literary work, since it is clearly structured by two different plots, whose relationship to one another is not immediately clear, but must be explained by the critic. In the first plot, which takes up most of the space of the novel, a group of technically skilled men – Union prisoners in the American civil war, escaping from their Confederate captors – crash their hot air balloon on a deserted island in the Pacific. Like Robinson Crusoe before them, they 'colonize' the island, reconstructing from the natural materials around them the technological products of contemporary society – including a windmill, a brickworks, a hydraulic lift and an electric telegraph – with the aim of making it another American state to offer to the Union after the war. This plot follows in detail the process of colonization undertaken by the group, led by Cyrus Smith, the 'engineer', who embodies all the scientific and technological knowledge that society has accumulated thus far. In the second plot, the 'mysterious' nature of the island unfolds and, towards the end of the novel, is made clear. The colonists are continually assisted by an unknown and benevolent being, whom they never see, but to whom various inexplicable acts of provision must be ascribed. Near the end of the novel, we discover that this has been the work of Captain Nemo, who escaped the whirlpool at the end of Verne's earlier novel *Twenty Thousand Leagues Under the Seas*

(1869), and after the gradual death of all of his crew, brought his submarine, the *Nautilus*, to port in an underwater cave beneath the island on which the colonists were stranded. We find out that Nemo was an Indian prince, who fought against British colonial rule. After a series of defeats taught him that 'might makes right' was the law of the progress of civilization, disgusted with human society, he became the underwater recluse of *Twenty Thousand Leagues*. On hearing that the castaways in *The Mysterious Island* supported the abolition of slavery, Nemo decided to help them. Having told them this story, Nemo dies, and a volcanic explosion reduces the island to a small rock, from which the colonists are rescued – again as a result of Nemo's help – and taken back to America, where they rebuild their colony in Iowa.

How does Macherey read this novel symptomatically? In the first place, the first plot, that of the scientifically founded colonization of the desert island, takes up and reworks familiar themes from Verne's earlier and best-known works, such as *Journey to the Centre of the Earth* (1864), *Twenty Thousand Leagues Under the Seas* and *Around the World in Eighty Days* (1872) – the journey, the exploration of the unknown, the scientific expert, the transformative power of technology, and so on. These themes, Macherey argues, express a contemporary ideology, that of man's conquest of nature by industrial technology. In the late-nineteenth century, modern man was represented in all kinds of discourse, from philosophy to public opinion, as a producer of technologies whose power to dominate his natural environment was potentially limitless. There was nothing, it seemed, that the progress of human science and technology could not accomplish – and if it had not already produced the means of achieving a certain goal, it would nevertheless do so in the foreseeable future. It is this kind of ideology, Macherey argues, that Verne sets out to express in the main plot of *The Mysterious Island*. He writes:

> Firstly, then, a general and explicit theme against which the work is continuously defined: the internal transformation of the social order by a process which is history itself, but which has now (and here arises the theme of modernity) come to predominate: the conquest of nature by industry. This is an easily identifiable ideological theme.
>
> (Macherey 1978: 165)

This theme is expressed, Macherey argues, in the distance Verne maintains between his desert island story and those that preceded it, especially Daniel Defoe's *Robinson Crusoe* (1719). Verne's castaways are a kind of modern version of Robinson Crusoe, a portrayal of how much more in control of their natural environment late-nineteenth-century men, with their advanced science and technology, have become. Whereas Crusoe has a shipwreck full of food, clothes, tools, weapons and other products of the society he has left behind with which to rebuild his life, Verne's castaways land on their island with almost nothing, and must colonize their island with its natural resources alone. Furthermore, Verne's castaways, especially in the person of the engineer, approach their natural environment armed with scientific knowledge of that environment and of how to exploit its resources. In these differences between Verne's and Defoe's castaways, Macherey argues, Verne has represented a concept of modernity – this is what Crusoe would be like nowadays, if, as a modern man, he were stranded on a desert island. It is precisely in this concept of modernity that we can see the ideological self-understanding of the industrial bourgeoisie of Verne's age.

If Verne has expressed this ideology of the technological conquest of nature in the first plot of *The Mysterious Island*, it is clearly not expressed throughout the whole of the novel. The second plot, in which the colonists are assisted throughout their colonization of the island by the mysterious force that turns out to be Captain Nemo, contradicts the ideological message of the first plot. Far from being able to retrace the history of industrial technology from the beginning, the colonists encounter a series of natural limitations to their project, which are overcome only by the external agency of Nemo. The island is not just a desert island, representative of the nature that industrial technology has exploited, but a 'mysterious' island, in which an apparently super-natural force supplements that technology. It is thus no longer clear what the 'message' of the book is. In fact, for Macherey, it has no message, except that which inheres in the incompatible relationship between its two plots. He writes:

> The book acquires its true subject, and also its meaning, from the fact that, as it develops, this scheme [i.e., the ideology of the conquest of nature] is overturned and even reversed. The line of ideological realizations is broken

> the moment it crosses the development of another plot, which seems *more real*, in so far as it compels it to acknowledge the persistence of another form of the fiction.
>
> (Macherey 1978: 218)

Macherey's symptomatic reading focuses on the sites of the contradiction between the two plots, which he argues represents the encounter of the ideology represented in the main plot with its limits – with the fact of its incompleteness as a representation of historical reality. One such site is the incident in which a chest full of all the things the colonists need is washed up on the island, apparently from a shipwreck, but which we later discover was stocked and supplied by Nemo. Although the essence of the main plot consists in its differentiation of Verne's castaways from Robinson Crusoe, in this incident they are returned precisely to the state of Crusoe, namely, dependent on the products of the society they have left behind in order to reconstruct it. Verne writes of the situation of his castaways:

> The imaginary heroes of Daniel Defoe ... never found themselves so entirely helpless. These men had abundant resources of grain, animals, tools and munitions drawn from their stranded vessels; or else some wreckage had washed up along the shore which allowed them to provide for the necessities of life. ... From nothing [on the other hand, Verne's castaways] would need to supply themselves with everything!
>
> (Verne 2001: 45)

As soon as the shipwrecked chest appears, however, the castaways' modern ability to exploit their natural environment with industrial technology can no longer be contrasted with Crusoe's primitive labours. Rather, they are reduced to precisely the situation from which they were supposed to represent an advance. The ideology of the conquest of nature expressed in the first plot encounters its limits, its incompleteness as a representation of reality, in this element of the second plot.

Towards the end of the novel, the second plot culminates in the colonists' encounter with Nemo. They hear his life story and witness his death. In this encounter, Macherey argues, the limits of the ideology of the first plot are most clearly revealed. Nemo ends his story by asking the colonists to judge the combination of anti-colonial struggle and social retreat that has characterized his life: ' "Now sir," he said, "Now that you know my life, what is your judgement?" ' (Verne 2001: 594). Cyrus Smith replies:

> 'Captain, your error was in believing that you could bring back the past, and you have fought against progress, which is ineluctable. ... We may fight against someone who makes a mistake for a cause he believes to be just, but we do not cease to esteem him. ... History loves heroic madness.'
>
> (Verne 2001: 595)

Macherey reads Smith's judgement of Nemo as a 'condemnation of utopia' (Macherey 1978: 226). He means that Smith judges Nemo, as a freedom fighter and as a recluse, to have lived in a fantasy version of the past, rather than in the reality of the present. He has lived as if the world were a place in which justice for the peoples exploited by the colonial expansion of the industrial powers was still a realistic goal. In reality, Smith judges, this is not so. The future – 'progress', as he puts it – consists in the continued colonial expansion of the industrial powers, as of the industrial technology on which their power is based. It is at this point, Macherey argues, that the ideology that the novel began by expressing confronts its own limits most forcefully. This is because Nemo is not only a freedom fighter but also precisely the kind of man of science that Cyrus Smith, who judges him, also is. Verne writes of Nemo, 'The man of war became the scientist' (2001: 591). In the novel's first plot, Smith represents the scientific and technological capabilities of the industrial bourgeoisie. He represents 'modern man'. And yet, at the climax of the novel, he condemns Nemo's technological exploits – his design and production of the *Nautilus*, and hence all the resources with which he assists the colonists – as a commitment to the past, and as a fight against modernity. In the end, Macherey argues, the novel's two plots contradict one another. Nemo conquers nature through science and technology, just as Smith does. Yet it is precisely this figure of scientific and technological conquest that Smith condemns for living in a fictional construction of the past. In the novel's first plot, the conquest of nature (in the figure of Smith) represents progress and the future of society; in the second plot it represents (in the figure of Nemo) an evasion of progress and the past. In the first plot, the conquest of nature is a fiction that is supposed to represent a reality; in the second, it is a fiction that fails to represent reality.

Macherey relates the internal contradictions in the form of the novel back to the ideological materials out of which it is made. The incompatibility between the two plots, he argues, makes clear that the ideology expressed in the first plot is precisely that, an ideology, a misrepresentation of historical reality. It shows up the limits of the ideology of technology upon which Verne worked in his novel, that there are historical realities of which it is unable to speak. Specifically, it shows that the industrial bourgeoisie has not achieved its social dominance through science and technology alone, as the ideology suggests, but rather that their technological achievements depend upon the historical conditions through which they were realized, the conditions above all of industrial labour and exploitation. Macherey writes:

> This is more or less what happens: Jules Verne wants to represent, to translate, an imperative which is profoundly ideological, that notion of labour and conquest which is at the centre of his work. In relation to the historical reality which it recuperates, this ideal is contradictory: real labour is alienated, perfect conquest is inevitably constrained by the conditions of former colonization. These are the real limits of bourgeois ideology.
>
> (Macherey 1978: 237)

What Macherey means is this. In the contradictions between the two plots we have discussed, we see an attempt to represent modernity continually fall back into precisely the terms from which it was supposed to be distinguished. The colonists were supposed to be modern versions of Robinson Crusoe, but they turned back into Crusoe himself, as they were continually assisted by the products of the society they had apparently left behind. Nemo represented precisely the kind of science and technology that was supposed to characterize modernity, yet he was condemned as a figure of the past. Indeed, Macherey argues, Verne's very choice to represent an ideology of modernity in a historical literary form – the story of Robinson Crusoe – indicates its dependence upon history. In the ideology of technology in which Verne, like his contemporaries, lived, industrial technology was represented as the characteristic achievement of modern man. What was not represented was the history of this technology – the conditions of labour and exploitation through which it was brought into being and continued to develop. When Verne put this ideology to work in his novel, however, these limits – the historical realities of which the ideology did not speak, and existed in order to keep from being spoken of – became visible, in the internal contradictions and gaps in the novel. Macherey concludes that the novel constitutes a kind of critique of the ideology out of which it is made. Verne began with an intention to express an ideology of technology, but he achieved a representation of this ideology as such. The novel does not merely express the ideology, in other words, but shows us its limits, and the contradictory relationship between the ideology and the reality it misrepresents. Hence Macherey concludes, 'The book finally shows us – though it may not be in the manner stated – what it proposed to enunciate: the history of its moment' (Macherey 1978: 240).

## THE CLASS STRUGGLE IN THEORY

Althusser's theoretical anti-humanism was condemned by the Central Committee of the French Communist Party in March 1966. In his summing up of the Committee's resolution, General Secretary Waldeck Rochet stated: 'Communism without humanism would not be communism' (cited in Elliott 1987: 192). In 1967, Althusser began a process of self-criticism, which was to dominate his thinking until the mid-1970s. He renounced the 'theoreticism' of *For Marx* and *Reading Capital*, by which he meant their overemphasis on the effects of Marx's scientific revolution in theoretical discourse. In these texts, Althusser had thought of Marxist philosophy as the theory of the difference between scientific and ideological discourses. From 1967, he redefined philosophy as the 'class struggle in theory'. This 'second definition' entails a new concept both of the practice of philosophy and of that of literary criticism. Both discourses are now thought of as politically effective interventions in the field of cultural practice, which serve the interests either of the exploiting or of the exploited classes in the society in which they are practised.

Althusser sets out this new position most fully in his 'Reply to John Lewis (Self-Criticism)' (1972). As he had done in *For Marx*, Althusser begins this essay with a brief account of the political situation in which he writes. Philosophy, he argues, has a role to play in this situation. Why? Because '*philosophy is, in the last instance, class struggle in the field of theory*' (*ESC*: 37). This statement has two footnotes, in which Althusser stresses the meaning of the qualification, 'in the last instance'. He means that philosophy is not only the product of the class struggle. Rather, according to the logic of his theory of overdetermination, it is the product of the complex and mutually determining levels of social practice in which it is produced, among which the political practice of class struggle is dominant. He derives this formulation from Engels, who writes in the preface to *The Peasant War in Germany* (1874) that there are three forms of class struggle: economic, political and theoretical. The name of the class struggle in the field of theory, Althusser, writes, is philosophy. He exemplifies what he means with his responses to the British Communist John Lewis. He isolates the humanist positions on which Lewis bases his interpretation of Marx, and compares them to his own interpretation of the positions of 'Marxist-Leninist philosophy'. In each case, Althusser counterposes an anti-humanist thesis to the humanist thesis of Lewis. This process of counterposition, he goes on to explain, is precisely what he means by class struggle in theory.

Philosophical positions, he argues – all philosophical positions, including hs own and those of Lewis – have specific effects in all the other practices that comprise a social formation. In particular, they have effects in political practice and in scientific practice. In the sciences, Althusser argues – including human sciences like literary studies – philosophical positions either advance that science as a science or they hold back its progress as a science by reconstituting it as an ideology. It is dialectical materialism, or 'Marxist philosophy', that determines the extent to which a discourse that describes itself as a science really is one or not. Given a Marxist concept of the scientific status of a given discourse, philosophical theses, both as philosophers articulate them in the practice of philosophy and as scientists more or less consciously appeal to them in the practice of science, either advance that science as such or return it to the pre-scientific status of an ideology. Althusser writes:

> That is how, in the end, philosophy 'works' in the sciences. *Either* it helps them to produce new scientific knowledge, *or* it tries to wipe out these advances and drag humanity back to a time when the sciences did not exist.
> (*ESC*: 61)

Humanism is a philosophy that holds back the science of history. Once Marx had founded the problematic of historical materialism by breaking with the ideology of humanism, it was possible to produce a scientific knowledge of history. Marxist humanists such as John Lewis, however, retard the process of this scientific knowledge by attempting to understand historical phenomena in terms of the pre-scientific philosophy of humanism. In the second place, Althusser argues, philosophical theses have political effects. They serve the interest either of an exploiting class or of an exploited class. Althusser takes as an example Lewis's humanist thesis, 'It is man who makes history', in comparison with the truly Marxist theses, 'It is the masses who make history' and 'The class struggle is the motor of history'. Lewis's thesis serves those whose interest it is to talk about 'man', rather than about the 'masses', 'classes' or 'class struggle', namely the bourgeoisie. It tends, Althusser argues, to give workers the illusion that they are all-powerful as men, whereas in reality they are controlled as workers by the bourgeoisie. It distracts them from the fact that their power to resist this control consists not in their humanity, but in their organization as a class. He writes:

> On the one hand, therefore, we have a philosophical Thesis which, directly or indirectly, serves the political interests of the bourgeoisie. ... On the other hand we have Theses which directly help the working class to understand its role, its conditions of existence, of exploitation and of struggle, which help it to create organizations which will lead the struggle of all exploited people to seize state power from the bourgeoisie.
> (*ESC*: 64)

Althusser even re-interprets his account of Marx's epistemological break in the light of the concept of class struggle in theory. Rather than a single complete rejection of the ideology of humanism, Althusser comes to understand the break as the long, protracted and difficult process in which Marx, bourgeois by class origin, came to adopt a proletarian class position in theory. The entire history of philosophy, Althusser argues, is in the last instance the history of the struggle at the level of theory between positions which serve the exploiting classes and positions which serve the exploited classes.

Almost all the literary criticism indebted to Althusser has either worked through the logic of the concept of symptomatic reading, as Macherey has done, or that of the theory of Ideological State Apparatuses, which we will discuss in the next chapter. Little has been made of the second definition of philosophy as class struggle in theory. Nevertheless, this definition, which Althusser maintained until the end of his life, clearly has implications for the practice of literary criticism. In the first place, it means that literary criticism is a site of class struggle in theory. Criticism is always practised, more or less consciously, on the basis of a series of first principles, which have directly political effects in the social formation in which it is practised. The question is only in whose interests it is effective. Marxist criticism, according to Althusser's second definition, consists in the production of a discourse on literature that derives from positions that serve proletarian class interests. In *Formalism and Marxism* (1979), Tony Bennett formulates this kind of argument in the course of a critique of Althusser's literary theory. The political effect of a literary text, he argues, does not inhere in its relationship to the ideology in which it was produced, as Macherey claims, but follows from the way in which it is *re-produced* by literary criticism, and the other social institutions and practices – such as the education system, the publishing industry, and so on – in which it is appropriated. He argues that literary texts are always already 'occupied' by a host of interpretations. 'The question', he writes, 'is not what literature's political effects *are* but what they might be *made to be* ... by the operations of Marxist criticism' (Bennett 2003: 111). Criticism, that is, is a 'pre-eminently *political* exercise'. It does not demonstrate the effects of a given literary text – whether it internally distantiates the ideology within which it was produced, for example – but rather *produces* them. Marxist criticism, like all criticism, does not show how a text functions in class society; it *makes it function* in that society, in the interests of one class or another. As Bennett writes:

> All forms of criticism are inescapably and necessarily active and political forms of discourse. They so work upon literary texts as to modify them. Their activities belong to those real determinants which influence and condition the life of literary texts within the real social process.
>
> (Bennett 2003: 115)

Criticism, that is, is an intervention in the field of cultural practices within which literary texts are situated that serves the interests of one or another of the antagonistic classes by which society is constituted. Marxist criticism, for Bennett, according to the logic of Althusser's concept of the class struggle in theory, is an intervention in the field of cultural practice that serves the interests of the proletariat. It advances proletarian class positions in literary criticism.

---

**SUMMARY**

Althusser finds a reading practice he describes as 'symptomatic reading' at work in Marx's analyses of previous economists in *Capital*. In this kind of reading, Marx pays attention to the gaps, contradictions and other logical flaws in the texts he analyses, and shows that these are signs of another set of ideas at work in the texts, of which their authors are unconscious. This kind of reading, Althusser argues, is based on a theory of knowledge as a process of production. Economists before Marx had produced knowledge of certain economic facts, but were not able to understand or to name them in the terms of the ideological problematics within which they thought. Althusser's student Pierre Macherey works out the consequences of this theory for literary criticism. It follows from the science of history, as Althusser understands it, that literary works are produced from the raw materials of ideology. Although ideologies seem, when we live in them, to constitute a more or less complete account of the world, in fact, as misrepresentations of historical reality, they are necessarily incomplete. When they are worked up into literary texts, this incompleteness is shown up, in the gaps, contradictions and other flaws in those texts. A literary text, for Macherey, has no 'unity', as bourgeois criticism supposes, but rather consists of conflicting and contradictory elements, irreducible to the intention of its author. As his reading of Jules Verne's *The Mysterious Island* makes clear, scientific literary criticism focuses on these conflicting elements, explaining their relationships to be a result of the historically misrepresentative character of the ideologies out of which they are made. From 1967, Althusser develops his 'second definition' of philosophy, as the 'class struggle in theory'. From this definition, it follows that literary criticism is a political intervention in the field of cultural practice, which serves the interests either of the exploiting or the exploited classes of the society in which it is practised.

# 4

# THE POLITICS OF CULTURE: ESSAYS ON IDEOLOGY

Althusser's most influential contribution to literary and cultural studies has been his theory of ideology. In this chapter, I will examine this theory, beginning with Althusser's initial claim that ideology constitutes our 'lived' relationship to historical reality, or our 'world' itself. I will then examine his concept of ideology as an imaginary relationship to real conditions of existence, discussing the role of popular culture in representing this imaginary relationship. In the main part of the chapter, I will examine Althusser's most influential essay, 'Ideology and Ideological State Apparatuses' (1969), a significant development of the Marxist theory of ideology, in which he advances the claim that ideology 'interpellates individuals as subjects'. I will conclude the chapter with an examination of some of the ways in which this theory has been applied in literary criticism.

## AN IMAGINARY RELATIONSHIP TO REALITY

Althusser first expounds his concept of ideology in the essay 'Marxism and Humanism' (1963). In the course of this essay's argument that the only authentically Marxist view of humanism must be that it is an ideology, Althusser explains what he means by an ideology. This is his first definition:

> An ideology is a system (with its own logic and rigour) of representations (images, myths, ideas or concepts, depending on the case) endowed with a historical existence and a role within a given society. ... Ideology, as a system of representations, is distinguished from science in that in it the practico-social function is more important than the theoretical function (function as knowledge).
>
> (*FM*: 231)

Marx and Engels had thought of society as a structure consisting of three fundamental levels – the economic base, and the superstructure, consisting of legal and political institutions on the one hand, and ideology on the other. They thought of ideology as the sum of the forms in which men and women were conscious of the production relations and of the class struggle by which their society was in reality constituted. Althusser adds a fourth level to this concept of society, that of science, first among which is the science of historical materialism. So, by describing ideologies as systems of representation in which the 'practico-social' function is more important than the theoretical function, he means that there are two fundamentally distinct forms of discourse at work in capitalist societies – science, which provides us with real knowledge of those societies, and ideology, which does not. Ideology has a social function, for Althusser, but this function is not that of producing knowledge of the real historical conditions of society.

What then is the social function of ideology? In order to answer this question, Althusser draws on a symptomatic reading of Marx. Whereas Marx and Engels had spoken of ideology largely in terms of 'forms of consciousness', Althusser argues that this is language that still belongs to the problematic preceding Marx, in which ideas were held to be the reality governing human life. Although Marx developed the scientific concept of ideology, he continued to use pre-scientific language in describing it, because the process of developing the fully systematic terminology appropriate to the science he had discovered was a long and difficult one. In fact, Althusser argues, according to the principles of this science articulated elsewhere in Marx's work, ideology has little to do with consciousness. Rather, it is a profoundly *unconscious* phenomenon. Althusser writes:

> Ideology is indeed a system of representations, but in the majority of cases these representations have nothing to do with 'consciousness': they are usually images and occasionally concepts, but it is above all as *structures* that they impose on the vast majority of men, not via their 'consciousness'. They are perceived-accepted-suffered cultural objects and they act functionally on men via a process that escapes them.
>
> (*FM*: 233)

He means that ideology is primarily the kind of discourse that we do not consciously appropriate for ourselves, rationally judging it to be true. It is not the kind of discourse to which, having critically reflected upon it, a person makes a conscious act of assent. Rather, ideology comprises the stream of discourses, images and ideas that are all around us all the time, into which we are born, in which we grow up, and in which we live, think and act. The messages of the advertisements by which we are constantly surrounded, for example – the images of a healthy family relationship, of a mother's role, appearance, weight, hairstyle, reading matter, interests, and so on, of the ideal male and female bodies, of the ideal clothes, lifestyle, home, eating habits, entertainments, of the way in which we are supposed to think, look, and want – all these are examples of ideology in Althusser's sense. It comes to us primarily in the form of obviousness – common sense, popular opinion, what everybody thinks, what we take for granted. Western culture is better than Muslim culture; people should get married and have children, especially women; the British are fundamentally decent, tolerant people; hard work brings success. All these assumptions, insofar as they remain assumptions, rather than becoming objects of critical reflection, are examples of the kind of sub-conscious conceptual framework that constitutes ideology.

Althusser puts this most clearly when he describes ideology as the way in which people understand their world. Ideology, for Althusser, is the set of discourses in whose terms we understand our experience – it constitutes the world of our experience, our 'world', itself. The science of historical materialism tells me about the material reality of my existence in the complex set of forces and relations of production that comprise the capitalist mode of production. Ordinarily, though, I do not think of my life in these terms. If I am in business, I might think of my life as a kind of competition, in which I need to be more shrewd, intelligent and hard-working than all the others. If I am a socialist, I might think of history as a progression from an increasingly exploitative to an increasingly just society, to which my political activities, from picketing factories to selling newspapers, contribute. If I am a Christian, I might think of my life as a moral progression towards eternity. If a mother, as building in my own small way the kind of community fit for my children to grow up in. These ways in which we understand our lives, these stories we tell ourselves in order to make sense of them are, for Althusser, the ideologies in which we live. He writes:

> Men live their actions, usually referred to as freedom and 'consciousness' by the classical tradition, in ideology, *by and through ideology*; in short, the 'lived' relation between men and the world, including History (in political action or inaction), passes through ideology, or better, *is ideology itself*.
>
> (*FM*: 233)

Ideology, that is, constitutes the series of discourses, images and concepts through which we 'live' our relationship to historical reality. It does not truly represent either that reality or our place in it. Although ideology comprises the discourses in whose terms I understand my life, this understanding is a misunderstanding. It constitutes the world of appearances, the pre-scientific understanding of men and women's lives in society, of which the Marxist science of history shows us the reality.

There remains a relationship between the world in which we tell ourselves that we live and the world in which we really live. Althusser specifies this relationship as follows:

> In ideology, men do indeed express, not the relation between them and their conditions of existence, but the *way* they live the relation between them and their conditions of existence: this presupposes both a real relation and an 'imaginary', 'lived' relation. Ideology, then, is the expression of the relation between men and their 'world', that is, the (overdetermined) unity of the real relation and the imaginary relation between them and their real conditions of existence.
>
> (*FM*: 233)

In ideology, that is, people express their real relation to the system of social relations in which they live in discourses that represent this relationship in an imaginary or fictitious form. It is a representation of 'the imaginary relationship of individuals to their real conditions of existence' (*LP*: 153). In 'Theory, Theoretical Practice and Theoretical Formation' (1966), Althusser writes that ideology makes an 'allusion' to historical reality at the same time as it constitutes an 'illusion' with respect to that reality:

> We understand that ... ideological representation imparts a certain 'representation' of reality, that it makes *allusion* to the real in a certain way, but that at the same time it bestows only an *illusion* on reality. We also understand that ideology gives men a certain 'knowledge' [*connaissance*] of their world, or rather allows them to 'recognize' themselves in their world, gives them a certain 'recognition' [*reconnaissance*]; but at the same time, ideology only introduces them to its *misrecognition* [*méconnaissance*]. *Allusion-illusion* or *recognition-misrecognition* – such is ideology from the perspective of its relation to the real.
>
> (*PSPS*: 29)

Althusser takes the term *méconnaissance*, 'misrecognition', from the work of the psychoanalyst Jacques Lacan (1901–1980). In Althusser's account of ideology, it retains the connotation of desire that it has in Lacan's psychoanalysis. In other words, Althusser means that in misrepresenting or 'misrecognizing' historical reality, ideology expresses a wish or a desire. We misrepresent the world in ideology because we *want* to do so, because there is some reward or benefit to us in doing so. The nature of this reward differs with respect to the class position of the individual living within a given ideology – a factory hand believes in God in a different way from a factory owner – but in every case, in Althusser's view, ideology misrepresents reality because people want it to do so. He writes:

> In ideology the real relation is invariably invested in the imaginary relation, a relation that *expresses a will* (conservative, conformist, reformist or revolutionary), a hope or a nostalgia, rather than describing a reality.
>
> (*FM*: 234)

Althusser adds two important qualifications to this theory of ideology. First, he argues that since ideology expresses an imaginary relationship to reality for everyone who lives in it, it cannot be conceived as an instrumental discourse, which the ruling classes cynically peddle in order to deceive the exploited classes. He calls this the 'Priests and Despots' theory of ideology, according to which:

> Priests and Despots ... 'forged' the Beautiful Lies so that, in the belief that they were obeying God, men would in fact obey the Priests and Despots, who are usually in alliance in their imposture.
>
> (*LP*: 153)

In reality, Althusser argues, the ruling class lives its own ideology, just as the exploited classes do. A general does not send his men out to die for their country, for example, without firmly believing that it is their duty to do so. Althusser writes: 'The ruling class does not maintain with its own ideology, which is the ruling ideology, an external and lucid relation of pure utility and cunning' (*FM*: 234). On the contrary, the bourgeoisie believes its own ideology as strongly as the proletariat. It has to 'believe in its own myth', as Althusser puts it – that all men are 'free', free to work or not, free to hire at the lowest price possible – 'before it can convince others' (*FM*: 234).

Second, Althusser points out that although a society's ideology consists primarily of the ideology of its dominant classes, nevertheless the dominated classes also produce ideologies, which express their protest against this domination. It is in this sense that Althusser speaks of proletarian ideology or petit-bourgeois ideology as well as of bourgeois ideology. He writes: 'Within ideology in general, we ... observe the existence of *different ideological tendencies* that express representations of the different social classes.' (*PSPS*: 30) Nevertheless, although each class produces its own ideologies in this way, Althusser emphasizes that the ideologies of the subordinate classes are correspondingly subordinate discourses. Even the protests of the proletariat tend to be expressed in the terms of bourgeois ideology, because as the dominant ideology, these are the terms in which every class 'spontaneously' thinks and speaks. This is what Althusser means when he writes that 'bourgeois ideology dominates other ideologies' (*PSPS*: 30).

## SAVING PRIVATE RYAN

Clearly, Althusser's theory of ideology has implications for the study of culture. In practice, his theory of ideology has been influential in the study of popular culture, although critics have often objected that it is excessively pessimistic with respect to the capacity of readers to resist the dominant ideology at work in various cultural forms. I will now look at an example of a product of mass culture in which, as Althusser argues, a representation of an imaginary relationship to real conditions of existence is offered to the reader. I will take as an example a film that explicitly raises the issue of capitalist production relations in its attempt to efface their significance, Nora Ephron's *You've Got Mail* (1998). The heroine of this film, Kathleen Kelly (Meg Ryan), owns a small children's bookshop in the Upper West Side of New York. The hero, Joe Fox, (Tom Hanks), owns a giant chain of bookshops, which puts Kathleen out of business. The traumatic effect of this on her and her employees is emphasized – she says: 'I feel as if a part of me had died … and no-one can ever make it right'. Nevertheless Kathleen and Joe unwittingly fall in love over the internet, as they correspond anonymously in an internet chat room. Once Joe finds out that it is Kathleen he has been writing to, he pursues her. Just before the final scene, in which Kathleen also realizes who she has been writing to, the question of the relation between their economic relationship and their romantic relationship is explicitly raised:

Joe: If I hadn't been Fox Books and you hadn't been The Shop Around The Corner, and you and I had just … met.
Kathleen: I know …

In this penultimate speech, it seems that their position in capitalist society defines them. Their lives are determined by the material conditions that follow from their place in the system of production relations. But in the next scene we discover that this is not true. Kathleen finds out that it is Joe with whom she has fallen in love, tells him, 'I wanted it to be you so badly', and the film finishes with a close-up kiss. It transpires, in other words, that at the level of what really matters in human life, Joe is not Fox Books and Kathleen is not The Shop Around The Corner. Their places in the production relations of the capitalist society in which they live do not determine who they are. Fundamentally, they are individuals, centres of emotion and desire, who will be fulfilled above all by an emotional relationship with another individual. In Althusser's terms, the film represents for its viewers an imaginary relationship to their real conditions of existence. In reality, our lives are determined in every respect by the capitalist system of production relations within which we live. *You've Got Mail*, however, articulates the ideological claim that this is not the case. Economic relations, it tells us, are only a secondary and inessential part of who we 'really are'; it is our emotional relationships that constitute our most fundamental reality.

As a film, *You've Got Mail* has no aesthetic value. It is not even a 'good' romantic comedy. Just as the readers of romance novels interviewed by Janice Radway thought of novels that dealt too explicitly with rape before reconciling the heroine to the hero who had raped her as 'bad' romances (Radway 1984: 157–85), so this romantic comedy deals too explicitly with capitalism before effacing its significance in comparison to the love of the heroine and hero to be a 'good' example of the genre. As Macherey pointed out in his analysis of Verne, there are realities of which ideologies cannot speak. In the ideology of romantic love, economic relations can only be mentioned insofar as they are superseded by personal relations. This is the movement of *You've Got Mail*, but it is articulated awkwardly as the ideology flirts with its own limits. In the penultimate scene, Joe asks Kathleen, 'How can you forgive this guy for standing you up, and not forgive me for this tiny little thing of putting you out of business?' The romantic paraphernalia of the scene does not succeed in effacing the exploitative nature of the economic relations to which it refers. In the more successful romantic comedies, the economic lives of the protagonists are not mentioned at all. By never even speaking of those realities about which, as ideological discourse, they exist not to speak, they perform their ideological function all the more successfully.

## IDEOLOGICAL STATE APPARATUSES

Althusser's most influential contribution to the Marxist theory of ideology was his essay, 'Ideology and Ideological State Apparatuses', comprising extracts from a longer work on the reproduction of production relations. In this essay, Althusser addresses the question of how societies reproduce the relations of production by which they function. The question arises because production relations have always been relations of exploitation. How is it that the exploited allow themselves to continue to be exploited? In answering this question, Althusser develops the concept of the Ideological State Apparatus. In Marxist theory, the State is thought of first and foremost as the 'State apparatus', that is, as the sum of the institutions by which the ruling class maintains its economic dominance – the government, the civil service, the courts, the police, the prisons, and the army, and so on. Through a symptomatic reading of the history of Marxist political practice – in which, he argues, the State has always been treated as a more complex reality than Marxist theory has made explicit – Althusser claims that the State apparatus in fact consists of two overlapping but distinct sets of institutions. On the one hand, he argues, it consists of all that Marxist theory has so far recognized as part of the State apparatus – the repressive institutions through which the ruling class enforces its rule as such. Althusser calls this the 'Repressive State Apparatus'. He writes:

> The State Apparatus (SA) contains: the Government, the Administration, the Army, the Police, the Courts, the Prisons, etc., which constitute what I shall in future call the Repressive State Apparatus. Repressive suggests that the State Apparatus in question 'functions by violence' – at least ultimately (since repression, e.g. administrative repression, may take non-physical forms).
>
> (*LP*: 136)

On the other hand, Althusser argues, the State also consists of what he calls the 'Ideological State Apparatuses' (ISAs). These are apparently distinct and specialized institutions such as the following:

- the religious ISA (the system of the different churches)
- the educational ISA (the system of the different public and private schools)
- the family ISA
- the legal ISA

- the political ISA
- the trade union ISA
- the communications ISA (press, radio and television etc.)
- the cultural ISA (literature, the arts, sports etc.).

(*LP*: 137)

The fundamental difference between the Repressive State Apparatus (RSA) and the Ideological State Apparatuses (ISAs) is that the RSA functions primarily 'by violence', whereas the ISAs function primarily 'by ideology' (*LP*: 138). To be precise, Althusser writes:

> The (Repressive) State Apparatus functions massively and predominantly *by repression* (including physical repression), while functioning secondarily by ideology. (There is no such thing as a purely repressive apparatus.) ... For their part, the Ideological State Apparatuses function massively and predominantly *by ideology*, but they also function secondarily by repression, even if only ultimately, but only ultimately, this is very attenuated and concealed, even symbolic. (There is no such thing as a purely ideological apparatus.)
>
> (*LP*: 138)

What Althusser means is this. The RSA performs its social function, namely, maintaining the economic dominance of the ruling class or class alliance, through force or the immediate threat of force. If I resist arrest by the police, I will be forced into custody. If the courts sentence me to jail or to death, I will be forced to submit to the sentence. This compulsion is socially acceptable because I live in a series of ideological discourses that legitimize it. On the other hand, the ISAs perform their social function, which is also maintaining the economic dominance of the ruling class or class alliance, through ideological discourse. In a religious institution or a school, for example, I am taught to think and act in certain specific ways. Nevertheless, if I refuse to think and act within the limits tolerated by the institution, I can be given low grades, excluded from prestigious groups, have my grievances ignored, acquire a reputation as a troublemaker, and ultimately be banned from the institution altogether. The RSA and the ISAs, that is, work together to maintain the order of the state.

Although the ISAs are an apparently disparate body of institutions, Althusser writes, they are unified by the ideologies through which they function. In all the various ISAs – the media, sport, culture, both 'high' and 'popular', schools, universities, political parties, and so on – the set of ideological discourses at work is always dominated by the ruling ideologies, which are the ideologies of the ruling classes of the societies in which they have developed. Nevertheless, Althusser adds, the ISAs are not only the fundamental means by which a society's ruling ideology is transmitted. They are also a site in which oppositional ideologies – the ideologies of the exploited classes – are articulated. At the level of the discourses at work within them, the ISAs are a site of *class struggle*. Althusser writes:

> The class (or class alliance) in power cannot lay down the law in the ISAs as easily as it can in the (repressive) State apparatus, not only because the former ruling classes are able to retain strong positions there for a long time, but also because the resistance of the exploited classes is able to find means and occasions to express itself there, either by the utilization of their contradictions, or by conquering combat positions in them in the struggle.
>
> (*LP*: 140)

Althusser advances the thesis that in developed capitalist social formations, the dominant ISA is the education system. In the pre-capitalist historical period in Europe, he writes, the dominant ISA was the church, which performed not only religious functions, but also dominated politics, education and culture. It is because of this position, Althusser argues, that ideological struggle in the pre-capitalist period was conducted primarily at the level of religious and theological discourse. As the bourgeoisie rose to economic dominance, he writes, it wrested many of the church's ideological functions from it, with the result that:

> The ideological State apparatus which has been installed in the *dominant* position in mature capitalist social formations as a result of a violent political and ideological class struggle against the old dominant ideological State apparatus is the *educational ideological apparatus*.
>
> (*LP*: 144–45)

To be precise, Althusser adds, it can be said that, in developed capitalist societies, the school-family couple has replaced the church-family couple as the dominant group of ideological institutions. Althusser means that from the age of about four to that of about sixteen, every child in contemporary capitalist society is instructed for several hours a day, in the dominant discourses, techniques and customs of that society. They are taught the ruling ideologies directly, in the form of morals, religion and philosophy. They are also taught a variety of technical disciplines, including literary criticism. This occurs until the age of about 16 for most students who leave to become workers, until about 18 for most who leave to become lower and middle managers, and until about 21 for most who leave to become finance capitalists, managers, politicians and 'professional ideologists' like priests and teachers. Each group, Althusser argues, is educated in terms of the ideology that fits it best to its role in class society:

> Each mass ejected *en route* is practically provided with the ideology that suits the role it has to fulfil in class society: the role of the exploited (with a 'highly developed' 'professional' 'ethical' 'civic' 'national' and a-political consciousness); the role of the agent of exploitation (ability to give the workers orders and speak to them: 'human relations'), of the agent of repression (ability to give orders and enforce obedience 'without discussion', or ability to manipulate the demagogy of a political leader's rhetoric), or of the professional ideologist (ability to treat consciousnesses with the respect, i.e. with the contempt, blackmail and demagogy, they deserve, adapted to the accents of Morality, of Virtue, of 'Transcendence', of the Nation, of France's World Role, etc.)
>
> (*LP*: 147)

## IDEOLOGY HAS A MATERIAL EXISTENCE

Having put forward the concept of the ideological state apparatus, Althusser goes on to define what he means by the 'ideology' by which he has claimed that ISAs function. In the first place, he argues, 'ideology has a material existence' (*LP*: 55). He means that, although ideology consists primarily of discourse, and hence of the ideas represented by that discourse, it is nevertheless not an ideal phenomenon. Although it appears — within a certain philosophical ideology — that ideological ideas exist in the minds of individual subjects, Althusser argues that in reality this is not the case. It is not the case that, because of a certain system of ideas in which I believe (for example, the Christian faith), I participate in certain regular practices (like praying, going to church, taking communion, and so on), act in certain ways (Christian ethics), and even become a member of an institution (the church). Rather, Althusser argues, the institution, the practices and rituals precede and govern my system of ideas. This is what Althusser means when he writes that 'an ideology always exists in an apparatus, and its practice, or practices' (*LP*: 156). Even in the ideological notion of ideology, Althusser points out, namely that ideas precede actions, if a person behaves in a way that does not follow from his system of beliefs, then we suspect that he does not really believe what he claims to believe. Rather, we suspect that he believes something else, on the basis of which he really acts. An insight is hidden here into the way in which ideology functions, Althusser argues – namely, that an individual's ideas exist in her *practices*:

> Where only a single subject (such and such an individual) is concerned, the existence of the ideas of his belief is material in that *his ideas are his material actions inserted into material practices governed by material rituals which are themselves defined by the material ideological apparatus from which derive the ideas of that subject.*
>
> (*LP*: 158)

Althusser means that the Ideological State Apparatus logically precedes the individual member of it. It is not because we hold certain beliefs that we construct ISAs; rather, it is because ISAs have been constructed that we hold certain beliefs. The material apparatus – the institution, with all its practices and rituals – governs the beliefs of its members. Ideas are not the property of individual subjects, Althusser argues, but the result of the situation of those subjects, in class society, within a set of ISAs.

## IDEOLOGY INTERPELLATES INDIVIDUALS AS SUBJECTS

This reflection that the individual subject is only apparently the origin of his ideas and beliefs leads Althusser to his central thesis on ideology.

This is that 'ideology hails or interpellates individuals as subjects' (*LP*: 164). Before we unpack the meaning of this thesis, we first need to understand the meaning of the French verb *interpeller*, which can be translated as 'hails or interpellates'. In English, the verb 'to interpellate' is obscure, but in French *interpeller* is a more common term. It means firstly 'to call out to' or 'to shout at' someone, and secondly 'to question' someone, especially in the sense that the police question or 'interrogate' a suspect. In a police context, it means 'to take in for questioning'. So, when we translate *interpeller* as 'to hail or interpellate', these are the two basic senses of the term. The primary sense is 'to call out to', as one person might call out to another in the street. The secondary connotation is that, since this is an act often performed by the police, in questioning a suspect, then, when ideology 'calls out to' a person, it is to ensure that law and order are maintained. Althusser's French verb reiterates the point he made in developing the concept of the ISA – that ideology, like the police, works for the State.

By the thesis, 'ideology hails or interpellates individuals as subjects', Althusser means first of all that the most fundamental category of ideology – the category on which is founded all other ideological categories and concepts – is that of the 'subject'. It is in bourgeois ideology that the term 'subject' first arises, but Althusser argues that the same category was at work in earlier ideologies under different names, such as 'soul' or 'God'. The concept of the subject is one in which an individual human being is believed to be the independent origin of her own thoughts, actions and emotions. Althusser defines it as follows: 'a free subjectivity, a centre of initiatives, author of and responsible for its actions' (*LP*: 169). For Althusser, as we know, societies consist of a complex set of relations between the mutually interacting practices by which they are constituted. Individuals do not determine these practices or their relationships; rather, the practices and their relationships determine the lives of the individuals within them. The concept of the free and self-determining subject is therefore an ideological concept. In reality, each human being exists as an individual inserted into the complex set of practices (determined in the last instance by the economy) by which her society produces the material conditions of its members' lives. Nevertheless, this is not how we think of our lives. We think of ourselves in the terms with which philosophy has described subjects. We think that we have an identity, a personality, even a soul or a spirit, and that this constitutes our most fundamental reality. Why? Althusser's answer: ideology. It is ideology that causes individuals whose lives are in reality determined by their insertion in a complex series of social practices to believe that they are free subjects, the origin and source of their thoughts, emotions and actions. Althusser writes:

> Ideology 'acts' or 'functions' in such a way that it 'recruits' subjects among the individuals (it recruits them all), or 'transforms' the individuals into subjects (it transforms them all) by that very precise operation which I have called *interpellation* or hailing, and which can be imagined along the lines of the most commonplace everyday police (or other) hailing: 'Hey, you there!'
> (*LP*: 162–63)

Ideology addresses me, as it were, before I am even born, as I grow up and throughout my life, as an 'I', as a subject, as a site of identity, thought and action. This is what Althusser means by the term 'interpellation': ideology calls me into being as a subject, as if it were calling me by name in the street. It causes me to believe that I am a subject, although in the reality of the capitalist mode of production, I have none of the attributes of that ideological concept.

Althusser considers, as an example, the Christian religious ideology. In it, he argues, the 'subjects' of the ideology – Christians – are addressed or interpellated by the ISA of the Church. They are told that God exists, that He created them, that they are responsible to Him, and how to behave in order to please Him. They are even told that God became a human being like them, and that as human beings they will become like God. It is in terms like these that Christians understand themselves and act. Althusser discerns in this system of thought and practice several important aspects of the way in which ideology interpellates individuals as subjects. In the first place, he argues:

> All this 'procedure' to set up Christian religious subjects is dominated by a strange phenomenon: the fact that there can only be such a multitude of possible religious subjects on the absolute condition that there is a Unique, Absolute, *Other Subject*, i.e. God.
>
> (*LP*: 166)

The Christian ideology, that is, interpellates individuals as subjects firstly insofar as it posits another subject – a kind of primal and complete subject – with the concept of God. Within the Christian ISA, individuals learn to think of themselves and act as subjects insofar as they are addressed as such by the great Subject who precedes them. Althusser argues that this is a feature of all ideology, that it 'interpellates individuals as subjects in the name of a Unique and Absolute Subject' (*LP*: 168). It is difficult to see how, in other ideologies, a subject is posited that is 'Absolute' in the way that God is thought of as absolute in Christian theology. Nevertheless, Althusser means something like this. In every ideology a subject is posited as a kind of model or exemplar, on the basis of which the individuals within the ISA in which it is posited understand themselves and act. By structuring their understanding of themselves on the basis of the imaginary subject that precedes them, individuals come to think of themselves, and act as, subjects like it.

Second, Althusser argues that the subjects of ideology are 'subjects' in a second sense. Within the Christian ISA, the subjects are called upon to obey God. The subjects, as Althusser puts it, are 'subjected to the Subject'. Ideology does not just interpellate us as subjects in the sense that it leads us to think of ourselves as free centres of thought and action. It also interpellates us as subjects in the sense that Althusser defines a subject as 'a subjected being, one who submits to a higher authority, and is therefore stripped of all freedom except that of freely accepting his submission' (*LP*: 169). When we become subjects in the first sense of an ideology, we also become subjects in the second sense – we become obedient and unresisting agents of the mode of production within which the ISAs to which we belong function. As Althusser puts it, the subjects of ideology 'work all by themselves' (*LP*: 169). We fulfil our different roles in the system of production relations, which is a system of exploitation, without arguing and without imagining – indeed positively disbelieving – that there could or should be any other system of relations. Within ideology, although apparently free and responsible agents, we are in reality precisely the opposite – we are thinking as we are told to think, and acting as we are told to act, in the interests of the economic dominance of the ruling class. Althusser writes:

> The individual *is interpellated as a (free) subject in order that he shall submit freely to the commandments of the Subject, i.e. in order that he shall (freely) accept his subjection*, i.e. in order that he shall make the gestures and actions of his subjection 'all by himself'. *There are no subjects except by and for their subjection*. That is why they 'work all by themselves'.
>
> (*LP*: 169)

## THE SUBJECTS OF REALISM

Althusserian literary critics have emphasized the role of realist fiction in interpellating individuals as subjects. In *Critical Practice* (1980), Catherine Belsey offers a series of readings of nineteenth-century realist novels, emphasizing the ways in which these novels perform the ideological function of interpellating their readers as subjects. As Belsey acknowledges, a caveat is necessary here. It is not the novels in themselves that interpellate their readers – novels do not exist 'in themselves', isolated from their cultural context. Rather, we read them within the cultural and the educational ISAs, whose norms and conventions on the one hand produce them as valuable objects of consumption and investigation, and on the other constitute the terms within which it seems obvious or right to read them. So if realist fiction has an ideological effect within the ISAs of capitalist society, it is because the ideology at work in the practices that constitute these ISAs leads us to produce this effect from it.

How do realist novels interpellate us, from within the ideological codes in whose terms we read them, as subjects? In the first place,

Belsey argues, they offer themselves for interpretation on the principle that it is above all character that governs social action:

> Classic realism tends to offer as the 'obvious' basis of its intelligibility the assumption that character, unified and coherent, is the source of action. Subjectivity is a major – perhaps the major – theme of classic realism.
>
> (Belsey 1980: 73)

The characters of realism offer themselves to their readers as examples of Althusser's 'Absolute Subject' in the cultural ISA. They call to us, as it were, to think of ourselves as characters like them, stable, unified, and above all authors of our own actions. In reading the stories of characters such as Jane Eyre or David Copperfield, I come to think of myself as a character whose own history progresses in a similarly meaningful way. I come to think of myself as the centre of my own history. Belsey points out that in earlier literary forms, such as Elizabethan drama, pairs of characters often appear who are barely distinguishable from one another. Their destinies, as she puts it, are the only respects in which they differ. In realist fiction, on the other hand, when pairs of characters appear, it is more often to show that their destinies are a result precisely of their individual personalities. In *Middlemarch*, for example, when Dorothea Brooke rejects Sir James Chettam but her sister Celia marries him, these actions follow from the difference in their characters that George Eliot devotes considerable space to describing. In reading the story of characters like these, I come to think of my own character as a similarly determining force in my own life.

In the second place, Belsey argues, realist fiction interpellates the reader by describing events from a specific point of view into which it 'interpolates' her, or includes her in the narrative as a subject. In *Jane Eyre*, for example, the reader is addressed directly as 'you', as a site of subjectivity equivalent to that of the 'I' of the implied author. The reader is very frequently located 'in' realist narrative as events are described from the perspective of an individual character, as in this passage from *The Scarlet Letter*:

> From this intense consciousness of being the object of severe and universal observation, the wearer of the scarlet letter was at length relieved by dis-

cerning, on the outskirts of the crowd, a figure which irresistibly took possession of her thoughts.

(Hawthorne 1983: 56)

Here the reader is required to make sense of the text as if from within the subjective experience of one of the characters. She is directly asked, that is, to take up the position of a subject. This is also the case, Belsey argues, as the narrative point of view shifts from one character to another, and from character to narrator, as invariably occurs in realist fiction. In this case:

The reader participates not only in the point of view of the subject of the *énoncé*, the subject inscribed *in* the utterance [the character], but also in the point of view of the subject of the enunciation, the subject who narrates, who 'shows' [the character's] experience to the reader.

(Belsey 1980: 77)

As the reader is required to make sense of the text from the perspective of the narrator, she reads as if from within the subjective experience of the narrator, in which all the disparate and conflicting perspectives of the characters cohere. The narrator of the realist novel is often described in the terms of Althusser's Absolute Subject, God, as 'omniscient'. When this is the case, it is precisely this kind of subject position from which the reader is asked to read. If there is an unreliable first person narrator, Belsey adds, the position of knowledge from which the reader makes sense of the narrative becomes that of the implied author, the subject of the enunciation that includes the unreliable narrator. In each case, the reader is interpolated into the narrative as a subject, in whose experience all the apparently conflicting events of that narrative make sense. She is thereby interpellated as such a subject. The ideological function of realist fiction, in Althusser's terms, consists in these devices of interpellation. If reading novels contributes to my belief that I am the centre of my own thoughts and actions, able to make sense of and determine my own life, then it keeps me from understanding that my life is really determined by my position in the system of capitalist production relations.

## SUMMARY

Ideology, for Althusser, is the name of all the discourse in society that does not, like science, represent the reality of that society. It is the way in which men and women 'live' their relationship to reality; it represents 'the imaginary relationship of individuals to their real conditions of existence'. In his most influential essay, Althusser argues that ideologies exist materially as a set of practices within an institution, an Ideological State Apparatus, or ISA. An ISA, Althusser argues, is an institution that functions primarily by ideology, and primarily by the ruling ideology in a given society. This social function is secured by the Repressive State Apparatus, which functions primarily by force. The university, the discipline of literary studies, the publishing industry and the various cultural industries, such as the cinema and the media, are all ISAs. Although also a site of oppositional ideologies, they function primarily to perpetuate the ruling ideologies of capitalist society, most fundamental among which is the humanist ideology of the subject. All ideology, even before the rise of the bourgeoisie, for Althusser, 'interpellates individuals as subjects'. It leads us to believe that we are subjects in the philosophical sense – free and responsible centres of thought and action – and, in doing so, ensures that we remain subjects in the political sense – submissive to the ruling class. By keeping us all, both the exploiting and the exploited classes, believing that we are free, ideology ensures that most of us do not become so.

# 5

# MATERIALIST AESTHETICS: ESSAYS ON LITERATURE AND ART

Althusser wrote many pieces of cultural criticism throughout his career, as well as an essay in aesthetics. In this chapter I will examine these essays. We will begin with the 'Letter on Art' (1966), in which Althusser sets out his account of the relationship between art and ideology, an account that has been criticized as itself ideological. Although this theory focuses on the work's relationship to the ideology within which it was produced, Althusser's cultural criticism focuses on works in which he discerns a critique of the ideology within which they are read in capitalist society. I will focus in this chapter on his most detailed works of criticism, the essays on the Milanese playwright Carlo Bertolazzi (1870–1916), on the German socialist playwright Bertolt Brecht (1898–1956), and on the Italian painter Leonardo Cremonini (b. 1925). In each case, Althusser sees a critique in the structure of their work of the ideology within which they are read in the cultural ISA.

## ALTHUSSER'S AESTHETICS

In 'A Letter on Art' (1966), Althusser replied to the Communist critic André Daspre, who had addressed the question of the place of art in Althusser's theory of ideology. In response to Daspre's claim that art provides us with a kind of knowledge, Althusser sets out the principles of a theory of art. In the first place, he writes: '*I do not rank real art among the ideologies*, although art does have a quite particular and specific relationship with ideology' (*LP*: 203). Althusser argues that art does not produce knowledge, in the way that science does, but rather that it 'maintains a certain *specific relationship*' with knowledge (*LP*: 204). Art does not provide us with knowledge, but with something related to knowledge. To be precise, Althusser writes:

> I believe that a peculiarity of art is to 'make us see' (*nous donner à voir*), 'make us perceive', 'make us feel' something which *alludes* to reality. ... What art makes us *see*, and therefore gives to us in the form of '*seeing*', '*perceiving*' and '*feeling*' (which is not the form of *knowing*) is the *ideology* from which it is born, in which it bathes, from which it detaches itself as art, and to which it *alludes*.
>
> (*LP*: 204)

It is only science, for Althusser, that produces knowledge of an ideology as such. Nevertheless, if art does not allow us to come to know an ideology in scientific concepts, it allows us to 'see' that ideology. It allows us to see it, as it were, from the inside, whereas science produces knowledge of it from the outside. A great novel, for example, does not gives us the perspective on the ideologies within which it was written that the science of historical materialism does. That science would, through detailed reconstruction of the complex social whole within which the novel was written, explain the nature and function of the ideologies that constitute its raw material within that social whole. The novel, on the other hand, shows us what it is like to live within the ideologies within which it was written. What Althusser calls 'real' or 'authentic' art, through a kind of internal dislocation, allows us an objective view of ideological discourse as such. It allows us to see, feel or perceive the ideology out of which it is made, *as ideology*, as one of the everyday ways in which we understand the world:

> Balzac and Solzhenitsyn give us a 'view' of the ideology to which their work alludes and with which it is constantly fed, a view which presupposes a

*retreat*, an *internal distantiation* from the very ideology from which their novels emerged. They make us 'perceive' (but not know) in some sense *from the inside*, by an *internal distance*, the very ideology in which they are held.

(*LP*: 204)

Hence Althusser can say that art and science both speak of every aspect of reality, but in different ways. He writes: 'The real difference between art and science lies in the specific form in which they give us the same object in quite different ways' (*LP*: 205) – art in the form of 'seeing'; science in the form of 'knowing'. Solzhenitsyn's novel *One Day in the Life of Ivan Denisovich* (1962) can make us see the experience of living in the ideology of the Stalinist 'cult of personality'. It can, as a result, lead us to criticize this ideology. Although realist fiction may have the ideological function of interpellation we discussed in the previous chapter, if it is authentic art, Althusser argues, it will also provide us with a critical view of precisely the ideology of which it is a product. It is only the science of historical materialism, however, which can 'define the means to remedy [the] effects' of the ideology (*LP*: 205). Art provides us with a critical view of the ideologies that perpetuate the exploitative relations on which societies are based. It takes the Marxist science of history to know how to change these relations. What literary critics need, therefore, is to develop a scientific discourse on literature. Such a discourse must begin, Althusser argues, with '*rigorous reflection on the basic concepts of Marxism*' (*LP*: 207):

> If we must turn ... to the 'basic principles of Marxism' in order to be able to [think] correctly, in concepts which are not the ideological concepts of aesthetic spontaneity, but scientific concepts adequate to their objects, and thus necessarily *new* concepts, it is not in order to pass art silently by or to sacrifice it to science: it is quite simply in order to *know* it, and to give it its due.
>
> (*LP*: 208)

Critics have objected to the concept of 'real art' with which Althusser's works in this essay. In *Formalism and Marxism*, Tony Bennett argues that, in common with earlier Marxist aestheticians, Althusser fails to effect an epistemological break with the ideological concerns of bourgeois aesthetics.

Althusser argues for the development of a Marxist science of literature, but, according to the logic of his own concept of Marxist science, he has not begun to practise such a discourse. First, the concept of real art, as opposed to 'works of an average or mediocre level' (*LP*: 204), depends upon values that derive from precisely the kind of humanistic ideology with which Althusser argues that Marxist science represents a break. Second, Althusser's very concept of art assumes the existence of a body of works with certain essential properties in common, despite the great differences in the historical conditions of their production. This is an assumption of bourgeois aesthetics, Bennett argues, with no place in historical materialist analysis, for which the conditions of production of cultural works determine them in every respect. This can be seen especially clearly in Althusser's subsumption of the category 'literature' into the more general category of 'art'. This can only be done on the principle that there is a set of properties which all art-forms have in common, despite their material differences as social practices, a principle that historical materialism rejects. Althusser's 'Letter on Art', for Bennett, remains within the pre-scientific problematic of aesthetics. If a Marxist science of cultural production is to be produced, he argues, it will not consist of a theory of 'art' or of 'literature' at all, since these are ideological concepts. Rather, it must recognize the 'full variety of cultural practice', of which the works designated by these categories are only a part. What is needed, Bennett writes, is 'a historically concrete analysis of the different relationships which may exist between different forms of fictional writing and the ideologies to which they allude' (Bennett 2003: 108).

## MATERIALIST THEATRE

In practice, Althusser's cultural criticism does not depend as heavily on the categories of traditional aesthetics as the 'Letter on Art' suggests. His first piece of criticism, 'The "Piccolo Teatro": Bertolazzi and Brecht. Notes on a Materialist Theatre' (1962), was an analysis of a melodrama, a thoroughly 'popular' form of cultural production. The Piccolo Teatro di Milano was founded in 1947 by Paolo Grassi (1919–1981) and Giorgio Strehler (1921–1997) to provide theatre for an informed mass audience. In the first part of his essay, Althusser analyses Strehler's production of the

Milanese play *La Povera Gent* ('The Poor People', 1893), by Carlo Bertolazzi, which the latter had intended as the first part of a trilogy entitled *El Nost Milan* ('Our Milan'). Strehler compressed the four acts of Bertolazzi's play into a three-act production, with the latter title. Althusser points out first of all that the play is 'remarkable for its internal dissociation' (*FM*: 134). The three acts of Strehler's production all have a similar structure. For the majority of each act, numerous anonymous characters interact idly. Then, in a few minutes at the end of each act, a tragic story is played out between three characters, a proletarian girl, her father, and the Togasso, the typical 'good-for-nothing' character, who wants to seduce her. Althusser sums up the play's plot in the first section of his essay. In Act 1, the scene is a cheap fairground in the 1890s. For most of the act, a mass of proletarian and sub-proletarian characters – unemployed, beggars, thieves, prostitutes – come and go through the fair's various stalls. Then, at the end of the act, 'in a flash, a "story" is sketched out' (*FM*: 132). A girl, Nina, is staring through a tear in the circus tent at the clown. She is watched by the Togasso, who wants to seduce her. She defies him and quickly departs. Her father Peppon, the fire-eater, who has seen everything, appears. In Act 2, we see the same idle interaction between anonymous sub-proletarian characters for the majority of the act, but this time the scene is a soup kitchen. At the end of the act, Nina reappears, and we learn that the clown is dead. The Togasso forces her to kiss him and give him what little money she has. Peppon then appears, and, after a struggle, kills the Togasso and flees. Act 3 has the same structure. This time, the scene is the women's night-shelter. When all the characters leave at the end of the act, Nina, who was sleeping there, remains. Her father comes to see her, to make her understand, before he goes to prison, that he killed for her honour. But she turns on him for having brought her up with such lies. She will pay the price and sell herself in order to leave the world of poverty and enter the other world where money and pleasure rule. Her father leaves broken, but Nina, knowing how to save herself, goes proudly out into the daylight.

Althusser points out that the production's three acts have the same structure and almost the same content. A long, slow 'empty' time, populated by numerous characters, precedes a 'lightning-short', 'full' time, in which three characters play out their tragic story.

Furthermore, Althusser points out, 'there is no *explicit* relationship between these two times or between these two spaces' (*FM*: 134). The characters of the empty time seem unrelated to those of the full time, giving way to them at the end of one act only to reappear in another form at the beginning of the next. This dissociation between the play's two times creates the strongest aesthetic response in the spectator, Althusser argues, and he asks how and why it functions within the play. His answer: 'The answer lies in a paradox: the true relationship is constituted precisely by the absence of relations' (*FM*: 135). In the play's first temporal mode, the time of the 'chronicle', as Althusser puts it, the existence of the Milanese sub-proletariat in the 1890s is portrayed. In the second temporal mode, the time of the 'tragedy', a melodrama is enacted. To be precise, the action of the tragedy is driven by the 'melodramatic consciousness' of Nina's father: his daughter's honour is compromised, and he has therefore to avenge this violation with blood. It is the absence of a relationship between the melodramatic consciousness and the existence of the Milanese sub-proletariat, Althusser argues, that is represented by the structure of the play.

What is the significance of this absent relationship? In the first place, Althusser argues, we need to understand the meaning of the empty time of the chronicle of wretched existence that constitutes the majority of the play. The point of the theatrical devices that represent its emptiness, he writes, is to portray the content of this time:

> It is a time in which nothing happens, a time without hope or future, a time in which even the past is fixed in repetition ... and the future is hardly groped for in the political stammerings of the labourers building the factory. ... In a word, a stationary time in which nothing resembling History can yet happen, an empty time, accepted as empty: the time of their situation itself.
>
> (*FM*: 136)

There is no *history* in the time of the play's sub-proletariat; they have no control over or agency in their lives, nor even the ideological illusion of such control or agency. They are pawns in a game played by others – the bourgeoisie – they know it, and they have no hope that it will ever change. In the time of the tragedy, on the other hand, this is no longer the case. Here we have a time in which 'some history must take place', which produces its own development by its own internal conflicts – the conflicts between Nina, her father and the Togasso. Because it generates its own history through this process of conflict, it is what Althusser calls a 'dialectical time'. (*FM*: 137). So the opposition between the two temporal modes of Bertolazzi's play can be summed up like this:

> On the one hand, a non-dialectical time, in which nothing happens, a time with no internal necessity forcing it into action; on the other, a dialectical time (that of conflict) induced by its internal contradictions to produce its development and result.
>
> (*FM*: 138)

The paradox of *El Nost Milan*, Althusser writes, is that the dialectic in it – that conflict between the characters that generates its plot – is acted only at the edges of the play, in one corner of the stage and at the end of each act. The reason for this, he argues, is that 'it is nothing but the dialectic of a consciousness' (*FM*: 138), that of Nina's father. For Althusser, consciousness has no independent existence, but is determined by the complex structure of social practices within which it exists. Hence, if it is to produce a real dialectic – a plot, that is, that authentically represents social reality – the play must criticize the dialectic that exists only in the consciousness of one of its characters. In Althusser's view, this is precisely what occurs.

Nina's father's consciousness is melodramatic. He drives the plot of the story of Nina, himself and the Togasso by the ideological concepts in which he lives (purity, innocence, honour, revenge), which are the components of melodrama. In *The Holy Family* (1845), Marx criticized the ways in which Eugène Sue's sentimental novel, *Les Mystères de Paris* (1843), represented the lives of its proletarian characters in the terms of bourgeois religious and moral ideas foreign to the reality of these lives. Althusser argues that the same is true of the melodramatic ideas in whose terms Nina's father understands the relationships between her, himself and the Togasso. They are foreign to the lives these characters materially live. He writes:

> The dialectic of the melodramatic consciousness is only possible at this price: this consciousness must be borrowed from outside (from the world of the alibis, sublimations and lies of bourgeois morality), and it must still be lived as *the* consciousness of a condition (that of the poor), even though this condition is radically foreign to the consciousness.
>
> (*FM*: 140)

The plot driven by Nina's father, then, insofar as he lives his melodramatic ideology as the reality of his place in society, can have no relation at all to the 'chronicle' parts of the play in which the real social relations of his class are represented. This is the meaning of the absence of relationship between the play's two temporal modes, Althusser argues. It shows that the ideology that governs the movement of the tragic plot has no relationship to the real social relations in which the play's characters live, and which are represented in the time of the chronicle. The dialectic of the tragic plot, Althusser writes, 'turns in a void, since it is only the dialectic of the void, cut off from the real world forever' (*FM*: 140).

In Eugène Sue's novel, there was no internal critique of the ideology in whose terms the characters' lives were represented. This is not the case in Bertolazzi's play, however. As Althusser writes: 'In the end, the last scene does give an answer to the paradox of the play and of its structure' (*FM*: 140). When, at the end of the play, Nina turns on her father for bringing her up in a system of illusions and lies, she criticizes and breaks from his melodramatic ideology. She breaks from the tragic plot which it has driven, choosing to enter the real world, however exploitative, rather than to remain within the limits of her father's ideology. Althusser writes:

> This dialectic, which only comes into its own at the extremities of the stage, in the aisles of a story it never succeeds in invading or dominating, is a very exact image for the quasi-null relation of a false consciousness to a real situation.
>
> (*FM*: 140)

In the end, he means, the tragic plot, although apparently the real story of the play, is in fact quite the opposite. The play shows us that it is a false story, driven by ideology. The world into which Nina walks at the end of the play is precisely the world that includes the time of the chronicle –

the real world, which produces both the poverty we see in the empty time and the ideological consciousness of this poverty that governs the tragic time. The play shows us, Althusser argues, that ideology can be thought of as false consciousness of the real world, which is instead governed by the exploitative production relations of capitalism. He writes:

> And this is what Marx said when he rejected the false dialectic of consciousness, even of popular consciousness, in favour of experience and study of the other world, the world of Capital.
>
> (*FM*: 141)

This is why Althusser calls Strehler's production of Bertolazzi's play an example of 'materialist' theatre. Like Marx's work, the play rejects the ideological forms in which people are spontaneously conscious of the social reality in which they live, showing that this reality is altogether different to its ideological misrepresentations. Like Marx, it shows that the reality of social relations explodes the apparent coherence of the ideologies that they produce.

## THE STRUCTURE OF ALIENATION

The claim that it is the structure of Bertolazzi's play that makes the strongest impression on the audience leads Althusser to a reflection on the theory of the 'alienation-effect' developed by the Marxist playwright Bertolt Brecht. In modern capitalist society, Brecht argues, the theatre has become a branch of the entertainment industry, in which the audience 'hand in their hat at the cloakroom and with it...their normal behaviour' (Brecht 1964: 39). The audience leaves the world of everyday life from which it has come to the theatre, and for a few hours lives in the different, imaginary world played out on stage. By creating the illusion of another world into which the spectators can project themselves, Brecht argues, the theatre provides them with an evening's entertainment, from which they return, unchanged, into the real world. Brecht, by contrast, aimed to produce plays in which 'the spectator, instead of being enabled to have an experience, is forced as it were to cast his vote' (Brecht 1964: 39). Instead of seeing the world played out on the stage as natural or inevitable, Brecht wanted his audiences to see it as historical, contingent and changeable. This is how men have made the world thus far, Brecht's plays tell the audience, but it can be done differently. It is with this attitude that they return to the real world. Brecht achieves this goal with an array of staging, acting and writing devices he describes as 'alienation-effects', whose aim is to show what is represented on stage in an unfamiliar way, so as 'to free socially conditioned phenomena from that stamp of familiarity which protects them against our grasp today' (Brecht 1964: 192). Whereas Marx had described the alienation (his term was *Entfremdung*) of the worker from himself and from the product of his work under capitalism, Brecht looks to achieve a different kind of alienation (his term is *Verfremdung*) in his theatre audiences from the ideology in whose terms they understand their lives in capitalist society.

Althusser argues that it is above all the structure of Brecht's plays, in particular *The Life of Galileo* (1938–43) and *Mother Courage and Her Children* (1939–41), that produces their alienation-effect. He discerns in these plays a similar 'decentred' structure to that of *El Nost Milan*. Once again, the consciousness of individual characters, in whose terms they understand their lives and act, coexists without any explicit relation to the historical reality of the social formation within which they do so. So in *Mother Courage* the 'plot' is driven by Mother Courage's personal tragedies – the loss of her children through her concern to keep her business going. These are played out against the background of the Thirty Years' War (1618–48), which progresses in the spaces between the scenes, as the titles in each scene make explicit. Althusser writes:

> The plays are decentred because they can have no centre, because, although the illusion-wrapped, naïve consciousness is his starting-point, Brecht refuses to make it that centre of the world it would like to be. That is why in these plays the centre is always to one side.
>
> (*FM*: 145)

The function of this structure, Althusser argues, is the same as that in Bertolazzi's play: the ideas in whose terms the characters understand their lives and act are shown to be illusions with respect to the historical reality in which they are formed. The structure of the plays represents both a critique of ideology and an account of its real conditions. It is this structure above all, Althusser argues, that constitutes the alienation-effect the plays produce in their audience. The spectator himself comes to the theatre and watches the play from within the ideologies in whose terms he is conscious of the world. As Althusser writes, 'What else is he if not the brother of the characters, caught in the spontaneous myths of ideology, in its illusions and privileged forms, as much as they are?' (*FM*: 148). Furthermore, Althusser argues, the event of coming to the theatre and watching a play is itself an ideological one. We 'recognize' ourselves in the characters we see on stage: they are 'characters' of the same kind as we imagine ourselves to be. They are examples in the cultural ISA of the Subject that interpellates us as subjects. Hence, Althusser writes, 'we are already ourselves in the play, from the beginning' (*FM*: 150). The question in analysing the theatre from the point of view of historical materialism then, is not, as Brecht suggests, whether or not the audience can identify with the characters. It is rather, what does the production do with this ideological self-recognition which is in place even before the curtain rises. Brecht achieves his alienation-effects, Althusser argues, less through his technical devices than through the structure of his plays, in which the audience watches the very forms of ideological consciousness that have brought them to the theatre in the first place criticized on the stage. Brecht's *Mother Courage* and *Galileo* critically analyse the ideology from within which the audience are watching the plays. Althusser writes:

> [They] displace it, put it to one side, find it and lose it, leave it, return to it, expose it from afar to forces which are external – and so drawn out – that like those wine-glasses broken at a distance by a physical resonance, it comes to a sudden end as a heap of splinters on the floor.
>
> (*FM*: 150)

It is through their experience of the illusory relationship of consciousness to real history as they watch Brecht's plays, Althusser argues, that the audience finds these plays producing a critical relationship to their own consciousness. It is in this sense that 'the play is really the production of a new spectator' (*FM*: 151).

## ART AND IDEOLOGY

In 'Cremonini, Painter of the Abstract' (1966), Althusser analyses the work of the Italian painter Leonardo Cremonini. Cremonini does not paint 'objects', Althusser argues, or even human 'subjects'. Rather, the fundamental object of his work is the structure of *relations* by which what appear to us in humanist ideology as 'subjects' and 'objects' are really linked. This is what Althusser means when he describes Cremonini as an 'abstract' painter. In historical materialism, the relations between people and things are abstract – they are not immediately given to perception, but must be deduced by scientific analysis. It is precisely these relations, by which our lives are determined, that constitute the object of Cremonini's painting, for Althusser. In the first place, he sees them represented in Cremonini's work, from the early 1960s onwards, in the form of 'an exploration of *mirrors*' (*LP*: 213). Cremonini paints many canvases in which, in the mirrors of ordinary homes and elsewhere, men and women look at their images, which we see looking back. The circle described by this gaze in and back out of the mirror is often accompanied, Althusser points out, by the vertical lines of doors, windows, partitions and walls. Cremonini paints two kinds of structure alongside one another, that is, without apparent relation to each other. On the one hand, he paints the circle of the gaze in and out of mirrors. In most cases, these mirrors are themselves circular, but the physical presence of a mirror is not necessary for the representation of this circle – Althusser also discerns it, for example, in a view from a room through a window into a neighbouring flat, in which the neighbours are looking back into the room from which they are seen. The point is that the circle is closed, referring to no other reality outside itself. Althusser writes:

> This *circle* really is a circle: it is 'cyclical', it has lost any origin; but along with the origin it also seems to have lost any 'determination in the last instance'. The men and their objects refer us to the objects and their men, and *vice versa*, endlessly.
> (*LP*: 214)

The circle of the gaze represents men, women and things as individuals – as individual human beings and as individual objects. They have no roots in the complex totality of material, social, historical existence, but relate only to one another as subjects and objects independent of this existence. The circle is, in short, the circle of humanist ideology. Now, Cremonini invariably paints alongside this circular structure another structure of tall, heavy vertical lines. Althusser describes these as follows:

> The great verticals of weight, which 'depict' something other than the perpetual reference of human-individuals to object-individuals and *vice versa* to infinity, something other than this circle of ideological existence: the determination of this circle by its difference, by a different, non-circular structure, by a law of quite a different nature.
>
> (*LP*: 214–15)

In the structure of heavy vertical lines, Althusser means, which accompany the humanistic circle of the gaze, Cremonini has depicted the inadequacy of this humanism. He has shown that there exists a reality to which it does not and cannot refer. This reality is not itself depicted in the canvases – it exists only in the *differences* between the objects and structures that are painted. It is impossible positively to paint social relations, because these are not given directly to sight, but have to be deduced by social science. Nevertheless, by painting a structure that can be seen to articulate the ideology of humanism alongside a structure with a different logic, Althusser argues, Cremonini has 'painted' the limits of this ideology. He has represented in form and colour the existence of a reality of which ideology does not speak. He has, as it were, painted the '*determinate absence* which governs' the people and objects present in his paintings (*FM*: 215), the system of social relations in which these people and objects really exist.

Althusser sees a similar critique of humanist ideology at work in Cremonini's human faces. In his distorted and deformed faces, Althusser sees a rejection of the ideological function of the face in painting. He writes:

> The humanist-religious ideological function of the human face is to be the seat of the 'soul', of subjectivity, and therefore the visible proof of the existence of the human subject with all the ideological force of the concept of the subject.
>
> (*LP*: 216)

In humanistic aesthetics, the face is implicitly the expression of the soul, the centre of the subject. The face must therefore have a recognizable individuality; it must express this particular soul. An aesthetic of ugliness, Althusser points out, is only a variant on this theme. Cremonini's faces, however, are characterized 'not by deformity but by deformation' (*LP*: 217). They do not express the souls of ugly, vicious or mad subjects; rather, they do not express the souls of subjects at all. Althusser writes:

> Their deformation is merely a determinate absence of form, a 'depiction' of their anonymity, and it is this anonymity that constitutes the actual cancellation of the categories of humanist ideology.
>
> (*LP*: 217)

When Cremonini seems to represent a face 'badly', or just to sketch its outline, for Althusser, he is showing that the individuals he paints are not subjects. Their faces have no clear expression, because they have no subjectivity to express. Rather, Cremonini's human beings are *anonymous*. Again, Althusser argues, Cremonini has painted a difference between human beings as they are understood in the ideology of humanism and as they really exist. In painting this difference, Cremonini has 'painted' the existence of a reality of which humanism does not speak, and by which his human beings are determined:

> They are haunted ... by a positive, determinate absence, that of the structure of the world which determines them, which makes them the anonymous beings that they are, the structural effects of the real relations which govern them.
>
> (*LP*: 217)

This 'radical anti-humanism' of Cremonini's work has a critical effect on the ideology within which we see it. Viewers of Cremonini's work do not find their ideological understanding of themselves confirmed. We think of ourselves as subjects, but we cannot see subjects like ourselves in Cremonini's paintings. The ideological effect of 'recognition' does not occur when I look at these paintings. If I cannot 'recognize' myself – which is in reality to misrecognize myself – in this way, Althusser argues, then I can begin to come to 'know' myself. He writes:

> Cremonini thus follows the path which was opened up to men by the great revolutionary thinkers, theoreticians and politicians, the great materialist thinkers who understood that the freedom of men is not achieved by the complacency of its ideological *recognition*, but *knowledge* of the laws of their slavery, and that the 'realization' of their concrete individuality is achieved by the analysis of and mastery of the abstract relations which govern them.
> 
> (*LP*: 219)

Cremonini's paintings, that is, show us aesthetically what Marx's economics tell us scientifically. If men and women are rationally to govern their lives together, they must come to recognize that the ideologies in which they live in capitalist society misrepresent the reality of that society, so as to be able to change the system of relations of which it consists.

## SUMMARY

Althusser argues that 'real art' is not an ideological discourse, but rather allows to us 'see' the ideology out of which it was produced. This view has been criticized for its dependence on pre-Marxist aesthetic concepts. In practice, Althusser values art which produces alienation-effects in those who read it from within the ideological codes of the cultural ISA. He argues that this alienation-effect is produced by the decentred structure of the plays of Bertolazzi and Brecht, a structure which he suggests is essential to materialist theatre. In the paintings of Cremonini, he finds a similar critique of humanist ideology at work in the abstract relations between people and things which constitute the absent object of these paintings. Like the scientific work of Marx, these aesthetic works show us, in their own way, that the ideologies in whose terms we understand the world constitute a misrepresentation of that world, rejection of which is the precondition for understanding and for changing it.

# 6

# POSTHUMOUS CONFESSIONS: *THE FUTURE LASTS A LONG TIME*

On 16 November 1980, in what he afterwards described as 'an intense and unforeseeable state of mental confusion', Althusser killed his wife Hélène, in the rooms they shared at the École normale supérieure in Paris. The post-mortem revealed that he had strangled her. Althusser recalls coming to consciousness of the scene, and hysterically rousing the École's doctor who, having established that Hélène was dead, drove him to the Sainte-Anne psychiatric hospital. When the magistrate arrived the next day to charge him with the murder, he was told that Althusser was mentally unfit to understand the legal process. A panel of psychiatrists was therefore appointed to examine him. Following their reports two months later, the magistrate declared a *non-lieu*, 'no grounds', meaning that Althusser was unfit to plead to the crime because he was not responsible for his actions at the time of committing it. He spent the next three years in mental hospitals, first at Saint-Anne and, from July 1981 at Soisy-sur-Seine, 40 kilometres (25 miles) from Paris. While there were periods after that in which he was able to live alone in Paris, in the flat that he and Hélène had bought for their retirement, he spent most of the remaining years of his life in hospital. Although he continued to write, his career as a public intellectual and a teacher was over. He died in hospital on 22 October 1990.

## 'BRIEF HISTORY OF A MURDERER'

Following the appearance of an article in *Le Monde* in March 1985, which referred in passing to 'juicy' murder trials of public figures such as himself, Althusser decided to write his own account of the events surrounding Hélène's murder, in place of the legal testimony he would have had to give had he been brought to trial. He wrote to a friend that he intended to write 'a sort of autobiography which would include [his] explanation of the tragedy, the way he had been "treated" by the police, the law and the doctors, and naturally what had caused it' (*FLLT*: 3). His friend Jean-Pierre Lefèbvre recalled that Althusser had sounded him out about a public gesture to remind people that he was still alive. He advised Althusser to begin with a humble project like a translation, as a kind of penance, but recalled that this 'was an opinion he didn't want to hear: he was in a manic phase' (Fox 1992: 4). In a few weeks, between late March and early May 1985, in one of the periods of productivity by which these phases were characterized, Althusser wrote the long autobiographical text *The Future Lasts a Long Time*, which he once considered sub-titling 'Brief History of a Murderer'. He collected and asked his friends to collect documents concerning article 64 of the 1838 Penal Code, under which he had been declared unfit to plead, as well as press cuttings concerning his case from France and abroad, and accounts from their diaries of the period. He also questioned his doctors and his psychoanalyst about the various treatments he had received. On the basis of this information, he wrote the text which, on its first page, he described as 'the response I would otherwise have been obliged to give' (*FLLT*: 13) to the charge of his wife's murder. He speaks of the 'tombstone of silence' beneath which someone declared unfit to plead is buried, a weight he wishes to lift with his own account of the events, which anyone else would have been permitted to give in public. He writes:

> I have decided to explain my actions publicly. ... I am doing it for my friends and for myself too, if that is possible, to remove the weight of the tombstone which lies over me. I wish ... to free myself from the circumstances [in which I found myself] as a result of my extremely serious state of mind.
>
> (*FLLT*: 27)

Nevertheless, Althusser did not publish the book. Its editors write: 'It is known ... that he referred to its existence on a number of occasions in front of several publishers and expressed the desire to see it published'. On the other hand, 'everything suggests that Althusser had taken extreme care to ensure that his manuscript was not widely circulated, which was the opposite of what he usually did with things he had written' (*FLLT*: 4). *The Future Lasts a Long Time* appeared posthumously in 1992, with the consent of Althusser's nephew and heir, although against the wishes of some of his close friends, including Macherey, who described it as 'a tissue of lies and half-truths' (Fox 1992: 4). It quickly became a best-seller.

## SELF-ANALYSIS

Althusser writes that the book is 'not a diary, not my memoirs, not an autobiography'. Rather, he writes, 'I simply wanted to remember those emotional experiences which had an impact on me and helped shape my life' (*FLLT*: 29). In the course of this account, Althusser gives psychological explanations of some of his philosophical positions. He rightly points out that such explanations have no logical consequences for those positions:

> It is no good looking for the ultimate and objective meaning of a particular philosophy in an analysis of this kind. Whatever a philosopher's conscious or rather subconscious inner motivation might be, his published philosophy has an entirely *objective reality* and its effect on the world, if it has one, is similarly objective.
>
> (*FLLT*: 175)

Nevertheless, the accounts of the subjective reasons that Althusser gives for his attraction to and formulation of certain philosophical positions are of interest in understanding the genesis of these positions. 'At the heart of it', he writes, 'was what I have referred to as the fulfilment of "my mother's desire" in a particularly pure and perfect, that is to say, abstract and ascetic form' (*FLLT*: 169). Throughout his account of his childhood development, Althusser had repeatedly stressed his mother's desire for 'purity', for intellectual rather than physical relationship. This, he believed, was the kind of relationship she had with her fiancé Louis Althusser before he was killed at the battle of Verdun in 1917 – 'They had a deep understanding of each other. Each was as sensible and as pure in heart – especially as pure – as the other. Both lived in the same realm of speculation and lofty ideas, far removed from any concern with that dangerous "thing", the body' (*FLLT*: 36). After Louis's death, his brother Charles, Althusser's father, married her in his place, and Althusser tells us that in his own name 'Louis', he always heard the name of 'him' (*lui*), the dead Louis whom his mother had really loved. Thus he perceived his mother's desire to be doubly spiritual, for an intellectual lover who existed only as a memory. 'Without doubt', Althusser writes, it was to fulfil the desire of his mother – to 'seduce' her, as he also puts it – that he became a philosopher at an élite intellectual institution and above all 'the author of a body of philosophical work which was abstract and impersonal, but passionately concerned with the self' (*FLLT*: 170). It is difficult to see how Althusser's work is 'passionately concerned with the self'. Presumably he means that the point of the Marxist critique of humanism is to bring into being the kind of human life that does not yet exist in capitalist society. His theoretical anti-humanism is more obviously 'abstract and impersonal'. According to *The Future Lasts a Long Time*, this fundamental characteristic of his work derives not only logically from a reading of Marx and from the kind of scientific analysis of history that Marx made possible, but also psychologically from the dynamics of Althusser's own childhood development.

He tells us that the same can be said of his conversion to Marxism. There were psychological reasons, he claims, as well as logical and political reasons, for his attraction to Marxist theory. Althusser stressed not only his mother's desire for intellectual relationships, which he experienced as a prohibition of his own physical existence, but also events and periods in which he broke free from this prohibition. This occurred especially in his relationship with his grandfather, during the periods he spent with him in the rural Morvan region, in central France. During a year he spent here, he was even known at the local school by his grandfather's name, Pierre Berger, because his own was too difficult to pronounce in the local dialect. It was as if he had become another person. Althusser writes: 'This was the exhilarating period of my life in which I finally acknowledged and had brought home to me the existence of my body, and when I truly realized its potential' (*FLLT*: 213). He also ascribes his ability to acquire physical skills like playing football and speaking other languages to this pleasure in bodily existence. When he encountered Marxism, Althusser writes that he was attracted to it as a theory and practice of physical life. In terms of his psychological development, it represented a system in which he could fulfil his own desire to exist bodily, overcoming the prohibition of this existence in the desire of his mother. He writes:

> When I 'came into contact' with Marxism, I subscribed to it with my body; not simply because it represented the radical critique of all 'speculative' illusions, but because it enabled me to establish a true relationship with plain reality, by way of the same critique of speculative illusions (both in terms of simple contact but above all by working on social or other dimensions of reality). In Marxism and Marxist *theory* I discovered a system of thought which acknowledged the primacy of the bodily activity, and labour over passive, speculative consciousness and I thought of this relationship as materialism itself.
> 
> (*FLLT*: 214)

Marxism was not only logically and politically persuasive to Althusser, he comes to reflect, but also represented, at the level of theory, the fulfilment of one of his most 'profound and longstanding desires': to live physically.

## READING THE SYMPTOMS

How should we understand these psychological accounts of Althusser's philosophical work? In the first place, we must note that *The Future Lasts a Long Time* is not a reliably factual account of Althusser's development and personal history. Althusser had already written an autobiographical fragment entitled *The Facts* in 1976, which also remained unpublished at his death. The 'facts' of Althusser's life in this account included meetings with Pope John XXIII and General de Gaulle, which Althusser tells us a few pages later were imaginary. He describes the wild fantasies of a manic period in the same past historic tense as the rest of the 'facts' of his life, including carrying out plans to steal an atomic submarine and to rob a bank. Even when he tells us that he did not meet John XXIII, the statement is followed by a dubious reference to Althusser's 'theft' of a retired cavalry officer, an affair that he says was of concern to the Vatican. Althusser's text articulates in these passages what he says explicitly in *The Future Lasts a Long Time*, that 'hallucinations are also facts' (*FLLT*: 81). This same movement in and out of fantasy occurs most explicitly in *The Future Lasts a Long Time* in a passage in which Althusser narrates having joined in the celebrations of the rural workers of his grandfather's community, but concludes the narration with a confession that it is no more than a fantasy:

> Faced with the truth, I now have to make a painful confession. I was not inside the great kitchen and therefore did not experience the wine-drinking and the chaotic singing at first hand. ... I dreamt it, that is to say, I had an intense desire for it to be real. It certainly could have happened, but for the sake of truth I have to accept and present it for what it was in my memory: a sort of hallucination of my intense desire.
>
> (*FLLT*: 81)

This oscillation between fact and fantasy occurs at a significant point with respect to the passages discussed above in which Althusser explains his philosophical positions in psychoanalytic terms. Marxism was the expression of his deepest desire, achieved at a high psychological cost, to live physically. It is in narrating his experience of the fulfilment of this desire among the rural workers of the Morvan that Althusser's text slips into fantasy. It is difficult to take his account of Marxism as a fulfilment of this same desire, therefore, as unproblematically factual. Indeed, the psychoanalytic context of the book (although he tells us it is a kind of address to a court of law, Althusser speaks primarily as if to his analyst) breaks down the empirical opposition between fact and fantasy. If this is how Althusser remembers the significant events of his life, then, in psychoanalytic terms, this is not only how they were for him but also how they now function. As he puts it:

> I intend to stick closely to the facts throughout this succession of memories by association; but hallucinations are also facts.
>
> (FLLT: 81)

The most difficult question in interpreting *The Future Lasts a Long Time* in relation to Althusser's philosophical work is that of the cognitive status he grants in this text to his own subjective experience. Althusser argued throughout his philosophical career that the subject was the fundamental category of ideology, but in writing his autobiography, he seems to depend on precisely this category. Citing Jean-Jacques Rousseau's *Confessions* (1753), Althusser writes that 'I can in all honesty subscribe to the following declaration of his: "I shall say openly what I did, what I thought, what I was." ' (*FLLT*: 29). In commenting on the psychological context of his philosophical work, he writes:

> All I seek to do is elucidate if possible the deep-seated, personal motives, both conscious and especially unconscious, which underpinned this whole undertaking beneath its outward and visible form.
>
> (FLLT: 169)

These statements depend upon the very concept of the subject that Althusser otherwise describes as the basis of the ideology from which Marxist science represents a break. When he says that 'deep-seated, personal motives' are the cause of the 'outward and visible form' of a person's actions, he means that an individual's character or personality determines his social action. Having systematically criticized the ideology of humanism in his philosophical work, Althusser writes his autobiography from within a humanist problematic. Even the concept of the unconscious in *The Future Lasts a Long Time* belongs to this problematic. In the thought of the French psychoanalyst Jacques Lacan, which Althusser endorses in 'Freud and Lacan' (1964), the unconscious consists in the trace of the subject's endless dispersal along the signifying chain. In *The Future Lasts a Long Time*, by contrast, it is a region of the

KEY IDEAS 117

subject's mind, whose contents can be reintegrated into consciousness through the psychoanalytic 'talking cure'.

Althusser constructs the position of subject for himself in this text, in both senses of the term that he distinguishes in the ISAs essay. Not only is the protagonist of the text a subject in the sense that his inner life determines his actions, he is also a subject in the sense of a 'subjected being'. He subjects to the law, writing the text as if in response to the interpellation of the legal ISA. In reality, however, the legal ISA did not interpellate Althusser as a subject. It interpellated him as a non-subject, as insane, and hence not fit to be considered one of its responsible agents. If it is an event of everyday class domination to be interpellated as a subject, it is an especially overwhelming event of domination to be interpellated as a non-subject. The ISAs, for Althusser, are sites of class struggle, in which oppositional discourses can be formulated within the dominant institutions. If these institutions interpellated him as a non-subject, however, he was excluded even from formulating an oppositional discourse within them. Several accounts of the problem of the relationship of *The Future Lasts a Long Time* to Althusser's philosophical work have been formulated. The Spanish philosopher Gabriel Albiac has argued that, in negating the premises of his earlier work in this late text, Althusser has enacted in it precisely the desire to which he attributes his murder of Hélène, the desire for self-destruction. He writes:

> If the murder that acted as the point of departure for this text destroyed – hardly in a metaphorical sense – the life of the author, the pages on which it is recounted – and the search to give the reasons for it – seem to have as their goal the completion of this tragic task: its object being nothing more than the destruction or, at least, the essential devaluation of the coherence of the body of work that preceded this definitive event.
>
> (Albiac 1998: 81)

Gregory Elliott sees the text as a 'symptom of the chronic manic-depressive syndrome which it hopes to exorcise through a public talking cure' (Elliott 1994: 181), pointing out that the optimistic conclusion to the penultimate chapter – 'life can still be beautiful. ... I feel younger now than I have ever done' (*FLLT*: 279) – shows all the signs of the manic phase which ended a few weeks later with another period of hospitalization. Warren Montag argues that the 'glaring contradiction' between the materialist principle not to judge a being by its self-consciousness and the project of autobiography constitutes the essence of *The Future Lasts a Long Time*. Arguing that the text articulates Althusser's failure to find the truth within himself, he describes it as a 'riddle masquerading as its own answer' (Montag 2003: 127). In my view, the source of the fundamental paradox of the text – that having spent twenty years rigorously criticizing the ideology of the subject, Althusser comes to write it from precisely within this ideology – lies in the question of interpellation. If it is an event of the class struggle to be interpellated as a subject, it is an especially powerful blow from the dominant class to be interpellated as a non-subject. *The Future Lasts a Long Time* represents Althusser's attempt to regain at least the position of subject, from which he could articulate an oppositional discourse in the class struggle within the ISAs, since even an oppositional discourse is denied to those whom the ISAs interpellate as unfit to constitute the subject of such a discourse.

## POLITICAL REFLECTIONS

In *The Future Lasts a Long Time*, Althusser also considers the political future of the Marxism to which he had dedicated his working life. In the late 1970s, he had written a series of essays in which he reflected critically on the contemporary state of Marxist theory and of Communist Party practice. In 'The Crisis of Marxism' (1977), he argued that the most fundamental form of this crisis consists in the failure of Marxist theory properly to have addressed the question uppermost in the minds of the working class concerning Marxism: 'Why and how did Soviet socialism lead to Stalin and to the present regime?' ('CM': 216). Not only has Marxist theory failed seriously to address this question, Althusser writes, but it is itself implicated in the problem it needs to explain, since the oppressive regimes in the USSR functioned precisely in the name of Marxism. If contemporary Marxists are to broach a serious historical, political and theoretical analysis of this issue, Althusser argues, it cannot be done by appealing to a 'pure' state of Marxist theory and practice, which existed before Stalin and which he single-handedly distorted. On the contrary, Althusser writes:

> The crisis through which we are living forces us to change something in our relation to Marxism, and in consequence, to change something in Marxism itself.
>
> ('CM': 218)

If Althusser argued in 1977 for a change in Marxist theory, in April 1978, following the defeat of the Union of the Left in the French elections, he wrote a bitter attack in *Le Monde* of the policy, strategy and organization of the French Communist Party, calling for a radical change in its theory and practice. He criticized the Party's authoritarian, 'vertical' structure, the leadership's strategy in the months leading up to the election, and its apparently greater concern to defeat the Socialist Party than to function in the class struggle of the French workers. He argued that the Party's structure had become precisely that of the bourgeois state against which it existed in order to lead the working class. The Communist Party, Althusser argued, needed to abandon these closed and authoritarian policies and practices if it was to fulfil this function. Instead, it needed to re-engage in 'concrete analysis of the class situation' in France, in 'theory which will not dodge mass initiatives and social transformations but which will, on the contrary, openly face them and impregnate and nourish itself with them', and in 'a policy of alliance of all working-class and popular forces' ('WMCP': 45).

In *The Future Lasts a Long Time*, Althusser reflects again on the future of Marxism, this time envisaging changes more radical than those for which he had called a few years before. In the first place, he tells us that he has lost faith in the goal of communist society. He writes: 'I am not sure whether humanity will ever experience communism; Marx's eschatological view of things' (*FLLT*: 224). What he is at this stage certain of is that socialism – such as it existed at that time in the USSR, Eastern Europe, China, Cuba and elsewhere – is not an 'inevitable transitional phase' towards communism. This ultimately deterministic view Althusser dismisses as a 'load of crap'. If the 'oases of communism' that even now exist in the world are to spread to the whole world, Althusser argues, they will do so in a way that 'no-one can foresee', but 'certainly not...on the basis of the Soviet model' (*FLLT*: 225). Rather, if there is hope for a world in which market relationships do not prevail – which Althusser calls the 'only possible definition of communism' – it comes from contemporary mass movements, many of which 'were unknown and not envisaged by Marx', such as liberation theology, the women's movement, or the Green Party. Althusser writes of such movements:

> Marxists are, thankfully, far from being the only ones striving nowadays to discover and tell the truth about reality. Without realizing how close they are to the Marxists, many honest people, with real practical experience, and conscious of the primacy of practical experience over mere consciousness, are already following them in their quest for truth.
>
> (*FLLT*: 224)

The crucial issue facing these mass movements, Althusser believes, is that of political organization. In order to be effective, they need such an organization, but have no viable model other than those of existing Marxist and socialist parties, which would lead to 'hierarchical domination'. Althusser's hope for future political change is based on his belief 'in intellectual lucidity and in the superiority of mass movements over the intellect' (*FLLT*: 226). If the intellect can follow the lead of the mass movements, he writes, it can perhaps lead them away from the historical errors of Communist Party practice and towards 'truly effective and democratic forms of organization' (*FLLT*: 226). It is in this sense that Althusser can say:

> I am an optimist, believing that Marxist thought will survive through thick and thin even if it assumes different forms – which is inevitable in a world undergoing profound change.
>
> (*FLLT*: 223)

Is Althusser inclining at the end of his life towards a post-Marxist position? Ultimately, no. In the first place, he is dismissive of the claims of postmodern philosophy to have moved beyond the Marxist problematic. He describes the contemporary situation as:

> A time when the leading 'hair-splitting' philosophy ... considers Marxism dead and buried, when the craziest ideas based on the most implausible eclecticism and feeble-minded theory are in fashion, under the pretext of so-called 'post-modernism', in which, yet again, 'matter has disappeared', giving way to the 'immateriality of communication'.
>
> (*FLLT*: 223)

His condemnation of postmodernism here includes the work of the French philosopher Jean-François Lyotard (1924–1998) and the sociologist Jean Baudrillard (b. 1929), both of whom began their work within the Marxist tradition, but explicitly moved beyond this tradition in the early 1970s. Althusser's criticism of Communist Party practice constitutes nothing like the fundamental critique of Marxist theory articulated by Lyotard and Baudrillard. Furthermore, while Althusser emphasizes the role of mass movements in *The Future Lasts a Long Time*, he does not see these movements as radically heterogeneous, exploding the logic of Marxist thought as such. He does not think in terms of the 'plurality of the social' (Laclau and Mouffe 2001: 5), on which the political theorists Ernesto Laclau and Chantal Mouffe base their explicitly 'post-Marxist' position. Having recognized that the new mass movements are not immediately explicable in the terms of Marxist theory, he calls for a development of this theory in response to them. He remains firmly within the Marxist tradition, but argues that this tradition needs to develop its theory and practice in dialogue with the popular concerns of the present. Hence he can write that 'I remain profoundly loyal to the materialism which inspired Marx, though without accepting it word for word, which I have never done' (*FLLT*: 223).

# AFTER ALTHUSSER

Althusser's work became massively influential in British and American literary studies in the 1970s, as *avant-garde* critics saw in his work the possibility for a critical discourse that was both truly scientific and politically radical. The French philosophies of the 1960s proved revolutionary in the 1970s for literary studies as they had traditionally been understood in Britain and the United States. The Leavisite orthodoxies of sensibility and the New Critical orthodoxies of textual criticism were exploded by a panoply of new ideas, directions, methods, terms and practices generated by the French philosophy of the 1960s, to which British and American critics quickly added their own voices. The French philosophies that proved most influential in English literary studies were politically radical – this was part of the excitement and the controversy that they generated – but it was Althusser who thought through the logic of Marxism most explicitly. Among the new canon of 'theorists', Althusser's work meant most to, and had most influence upon, literary and cultural critics on the Left. It is through this influence upon politically committed critics of the 1970s and '80s that he continues to be a shaping force behind the post-Marxist critical discourses of the present day.

## 'ALTHUSSERIANISM'

Althusser's work was appropriated and discussed by English-speaking literary critics in a very different way from in the French philosophical institution in which it was produced. 'Althusserianism' was a different phenomenon on either side of the English Channel. Étienne Balibar reflects:

> There probably never was, strictly speaking, an 'Althusserianism' as a closed system, or as a 'school', in France. Because in France, as opposed to England, Althusser's work preoccupied more than a small group of people, and consequently, was inevitably taken up from the start in controversies and contradictory tendencies.
>
> (Balibar and Macherey 1982: 47)

In Britain, because Althusser's work was appropriated by a theoretical *avant-garde*, 'Althusserianism' was a more recognizable, although still internally conflicted, movement. The Marxist critic Terry Eagleton describes the context in which Althusser's work became influential:

> The Vietnam, civil rights and student movements of the late 1960s and early 1970s; anti-imperialist struggle in the north of Ireland, and some major offensives by the labour movement: all of these events created a general political climate peculiarly conducive to theoretical debate on the left. Central to that renewed preoccupation with theory was the work of Louis Althusser and his associates, which was then becoming available in English translation. The appeal of Althusser's work, generally speaking, was that while it seemed on the one hand in its concerns with ideology and the 'relative autonomy' of superstructures to offer key theoretical concepts to those engaged in the socialist analysis of culture, it presented itself simultaneously, in its rehabilitation of the 'scientific' Marx, Leninism and in its vigorous anti-humanism, as in some sense politically revolutionary.
>
> (Eagleton 1986: 1)

Althusserianism, as Eagleton testifies, provided many intellectuals on the Left, in literary studies as in other disciplines, with a theoretically rigorous approach to their own field of study that seemed to have genuinely radical political consequences. It allowed Left literary critics both to work within the institutions of literary scholarship, and at the same time to criticize those institutions' predominantly liberal and humanistic ideologies. One such critic, Francis Mulhern, adds that the theoretical rigour of Althusser's Marxism appealed to the Left in literary studies insofar as 'a sense of intellectual illegitimacy was deep and persistent' (Mulhern 1994: 160). The British Marxist criticism of the 1930s, he writes, was a 'collective embarrassment' in its simplicity. The available European Marxist literary theory, on the other hand, was either 'incorrigibly schematic' (Lucien Goldmann) or 'prone to aesthetic dogmatism' (György Lukács). When Althusser's work became available in the late 1960s, Mulhern writes, there was the prospect of a 'new departure' in Marxist criticism, in which, for the first time:

> It was possible and necessary to broach the scientific, historical-materialist concept of art as an irreducible social practice, to imagine a properly Marxist theory of an unambiguously specified object.
> 
> (Mulhern 1994: 161)

## MACHEREY: LITERATURE AS AN IDEOLOGICAL FORM

Pierre Macherey continued to develop the project of a scientific literary criticism, based on Althusser's account of the science of historical materialism. As he pointed out in a 1977 interview, Althusser's essay on Ideological State Apparatuses had been a theoretical response to the 'events' of May 1968 in Paris, when student protests turned into mass strikes and demonstrations. After May 1968, Macherey said, 'We were forced to renounce all that formalism and culturalism which characterized our previous work' (Macherey 1977: 5). In the light of Althusser's ISAs essay, Macherey turned in the 1970s to an examination of the function of literature within the educational ISA. In 'On Literature as an Ideological Form', the preface to Renée Balibar's *Les français fictifs* (1974), Macherey and Étienne Balibar examine the ideological function of literature within the French education system. Following Renée Balibar's analyses of 'literary French', and its relation to 'ordinary French', Balibar and

Macherey write that, on the one hand, the school system is a national institution, unified as such by the national language used within it. On the other hand, within the apparent unity of this language, there are two distinct 'levels of teaching', each with their own kind of language. 'Basic French' (*français élémentaire*) is taught in primary education, whereas at the more advanced secondary level, 'literary French' (*français littéraire*) is taught. This division in schooling, Balibar and Macherey write 'reproduces the social division of a society based on the sale and purchase of labour-power' (Balibar and Macherey 1996: 281). There is one kind of language for the buyers, and another kind for the sellers, of labour-power in capitalist France. Capitalist society is divided fundamentally into two economic classes — the exploited and the exploiters. Balibar and Macherey argue that, in France, this division is perpetuated at the ideological level by the basic and the advanced, or 'literary', kinds of language in which these two classes are on the whole educated. At the same time as it is reproduced, they add, this division — and along with it the class division it reproduces — is effaced by the apparent unity of the national language. There are, Balibar and Macherey write:

> Two antagonistic uses, equal but inseparable, of the common language: on the one side, 'literary' French, which is studied in higher education [*l'enseignement secondaire et supérieur*] and on the other, 'basic', 'ordinary' French which, far from being natural, is also taught at the other level [*à l'école primaire*]. It is basic only by reason of its unequal relation to the other, which is 'literary' by the same reason.
>
> (Balibar and Macherey 1996: 293)

It is because it is literature that exemplifies the 'literary' or advanced kind of language in which the dominant class are educated in the later stages of the education system that Balibar and Macherey call it an 'ideological form'. 'Literature', they argue, is the name of that advanced kind of language which, in the French educational ISA, represents the superiority, and hence reproduces the dominance, of the exploiting classes. This role in the reproduction of the dominant classes as such constitutes the 'material function of literature' in society (Balibar and Macherey 1996: 282).

Within the educational ISA, literature itself is said to consist of especially valuable discourse. The nature of the value ascribed to it changes – it may be beauty, truth, moral, political or religious value – but it continues to be distinguished from non-literary discourse as valuable. This might be called the 'aesthetic effect' of literature – those qualities in a literary work that make reading it an especially valuable experience. Within the educational ISA in which literature is taught, however, Balibar and Macherey argue that its aesthetic effect does not in reality consist of this kind of experience. Rather, it consists fundamentally of the practices of literary criticism, scholarship and teaching that arise in response to 'literature', and which make up the institution of literary studies. There is an ideological circle at work in the concept of literature, that is – on the one hand, critical discourse arises, and along with it the institution of literary studies, because of the special value of literature; and on the other, literature is said to be especially valuable by this critical discourse. Balibar and Macherey write:

> We can now say that the literary text is the agent for the reproduction of ideology in its ensemble. In other words, it induces by the literary effect the production of 'new' discourses which always reproduce (under constantly varied forms) the same ideology (with its contradictions). It enables individuals to appropriate ideology and make themselves its 'free' bearers and even 'free' creators. The literary text is a privileged operator in the concrete relation between the individual and ideology in bourgeois society and ensures its reproduction.
>
> (Balibar and Macherey 1996: 292)

Within the educational ISA, Balibar and Macherey mean, literature functions as a means by which the dominant ideology is reproduced. Literary criticism appears, within the ideology of literature, to be an exercise of freedom, of individual opinion, taste or judgement. In reality, however, it consists of one of the practices by which an ISA – in fact, several ISAs: the school, the university and the literary ISA – is constituted. While these ISAs are sites in which oppositional ideologies can be articulated, on the whole they comprise practices in which the dominant ideology is reproduced. Literary criticism is an ideological discourse, one of the practices that constitute a series of ISAs. It is the function of literature within these ISAs, Balibar and Macherey argue, to generate this ideological discourse.

The 'aesthetic effect' of literature, therefore, is also an 'effect of domination'. Balibar and Macherey call the aesthetic qualities of literary texts an 'ideological domination-effect'. Within the ISAs in which literature functions, its 'literary' quality ensures the subjection of individuals to the dominant ideology. This subjection is lived differently by the dominant and dominated classes respectively, Balibar and Macherey argue. For the members of the dominant classes, educated in 'literary French', the literary language which they have become able to understand, appreciate and criticize, articulates their ' "freedom" to think within ideology', which Balibar and Macherey describe as a 'submission which is experienced and practised as if it were a mastery' (Balibar and Macherey 1996: 292). The working classes on the other hand, who on the whole do not read 'literature', and who in France did not complete an education in literary French, but mastered only the subordinate form of 'ordinary French', experience the literary quality of literature in a different way. Balibar and Macherey write:

> These find in reading nothing but the confirmation of their inferiority: subjection means domination and repression by the literary discourse of a discourse deemed 'inarticulate' and 'faulty' and inadequate for the expression of complex ideas and feelings.
>
> (Balibar and Macherey 1996: 292)

In Macherey's later literary studies, collected in *The Object of Literature* (1990), he returns to a more formalist mode of analysis. He retains the fundamental positions of *A Theory of Literary Production*, holding that 'literary rhetoric relates to the ideology of an era only insofar as it brings it into conflict with itself' (Macherey 1995: 237). Nevertheless, the object of his criticism is now what he calls 'literary philosophy', which he defines as the 'thought which is produced by literature', and which exists only in the form of the literary product, as opposed to a stratum of ideas which pre-exist the text and which it puts to work, as in *A Theory of Literary*

*Production*. Hence it can be described as 'thought without concepts'. Macherey writes:

> Literary philosophy is an essentially problematic intellectual experience: it consists in revealing philosophical problems, expounding them and 'staging' them in the theatrical sense of the term, and eschewing any definitive, or supposedly definitive, attempt to resolve them, put an end to them and suppress them with arguments.
>
> (Macherey 1995: 234)

So, in an essay on Victor Hugo, he analyses the figure of the 'man from below' in Hugo and other contemporary writers, describing this figure as a product of the 'historical imaginary', or the literary philosophy, of the 1830s and '40s. He argues that this figure, and its typical clusters of imagery, is a literary expression of a 'concern to recognize and to understand the emergence of a new reality: the masses' (Macherey 1995: 107). Macherey describes literary philosophy as the 'mythology' of a given social formation – an 'interpretation of its conditions of collective existence that is acceptable to all' (Macherey 1995: 108), which, like ideology in Althusser's earlier work, constitutes an 'essential element in [the] workings' of the social formation that produces it.

## TERRY EAGLETON: BEYOND TEXTUAL SCIENCE

The work of Althusser and Macherey was taken up most closely in English literary studies by Terry Eagleton (b. 1943). In *Criticism and Ideology* (1976) in particular, Eagleton works critically within the problematic of Althusser and Macherey in order to develop a scientific practice of literary criticism. He follows Macherey in arguing that a literary text produces the raw material of ideological discourse, adding by way of illustration that it does so in an analogous way to that in which a dramatic performance constitutes a 'production' of the text of a play. Furthermore, he argues, ideology is itself a production of a similar kind, of the raw material of historical reality. Hence he calls a literary text – as a production of a production – 'ideology to the second power' (Eagleton 1976: 70). Nevertheless, Eagleton is critical of Althusser's concept of 'real art'. He describes Althusser's 'Letter on Art' as a 'suggestive, radically unsatisfactory statement' (Eagleton 1976: 83). The concept of real art, he writes, is a 'notable evasion' of theoretical rigour, in which Althusser smuggles an evaluative judgement — that some art is real or 'authentic', whereas some is not — into a discourse that is supposed to represent the beginning of a scientific account of art. Eagleton asks:

> Is it *constitutive* of aesthetic 'authenticity' that the process here described occurs, or does it merely follow from works whose 'authenticity' is to be assessed by other, unexamined criteria?
>
> (Eagleton 1976: 83)

In the absence of a discussion of the criteria of real art, Althusser's account lapses into tautology, telling us in effect that real art is real art, or that works that internally distantiate the ideology from which they are made internally distantiate the ideology from which they are made. To Macherey's development of the argument, that it is by their form that literary texts internally distantiate their ideological content, Eagleton responds:

> To leave the matter there is merely to stand convicted of formalism. For if it is true that the text's relation to ideology is crucially effected by its forms, this is not the whole truth.
>
> (Eagleton 1976: 83)

Eagleton criticizes the desire he discerns in Althusser and Macherey to 'rescue' or 'redeem' the work of art from ideology. Their talk of art 'allowing us to see' ideology does little more than rephrase in apparently materialist language the traditional view that art 'transcends' or rises above mere entertainment or popular culture. We can see this again, he argues, in Althusser's position that it is in the reader that the ideological effect produced by the work takes place. Whereas, in bourgeois aesthetics, literature gives us an otherwise unavailable insight into reality, Eagleton argues, in the theory of Althusser and Macherey it gives us an otherwise unavailable insight into ideology. He writes:

> The liberal humanist problematic is preserved in different form: it is just that it is now ideology, rather than reality, which is revealed to us in a privileged moment of insight.
>
> (Eagleton 1976: 86)

Literary texts do not merely give ideology a form, Eagleton argues, since the formal devices they use to produce ideology are themselves ideological. The literary forms and devices available to an author in a given society are themselves determined by the history of that society. Eagleton writes:

> The text establishes a relationship with ideology by means of its forms, but it does so by means of the *character* of the ideology it works. It is the character of that ideology, *in conjunction with* the transmutative operations of the literary forms it produces or enables, which determines the degree to which the texts achieves significant or nugatory perceptions.
>
> (Eagleton 1976: 84)

Eagleton argues for a dialectical relationship between text and ideology, in which the literary text produces ideology in a series of forms, themes and devices available to its author within precisely that ideology. This is a mutually transformative relationship, he argues, which 'can only be grasped as a ceaseless, reciprocal *operation* of text on ideology and ideology on text' (Eagleton 1976: 99). The text recasts ideology in a process determined by the very ideology being recast. The objects of scientific literary criticism, therefore, are the 'two mutually constitutive formations: the nature of the ideology worked by the text and the aesthetic modes of that working' (Eagleton 1976: 85). A point that Macherey fails to develop in this respect, he argues, is that the relationship between text and ideology takes different forms. For Macherey, the text's working of its ideological content results in a series of internal contradictions and flaws. While this can be true, Eagleton argues, it is not always true. There are literary texts – he cites Alexander Pope's *Essay on Man* (1732–44) as an example – in which the contradictions in the ideology worked by the text do not result in an obviously self-contradictory text. In fact, Eagleton writes:

> There are conflicting ways in which ideology presses the text into disorder; and even here we must discriminate between disorder of *meaning* (or levels of meaning) and disorder of *form*.
>
> (Eagleton 1976: 94)

Eagleton's most fundamental criticism of Althusser and Macherey, from which all the previous objections derive, is that their concept of ideology is a 'totalizing' one, in which the internal contradictions by which ideologies are characterized are not properly recognized. For Macherey, ideology is a misrepresentation of historical reality which, although consistent in itself, cannot speak in its own terms about much of that reality. It exists precisely in order to keep us from speaking about it. Eagleton challenges this view. Ideology is not consistent or coherent in itself, he argues – rather it conflicts with and contradicts itself. It is built out of fragments of discourse that, precisely because they are misrepresentations of reality, fail to constitute a single, homogeneous account of that reality. Eagleton writes:

> Ideology ... has no such homogeneity: it is certainly *homogenizing* in tendency, but it nowhere, fortunately, has the success which Macherey assigns to it. Althusser's own work has grievously underplayed the degree to which ideology, as a terrain of class struggle, is itself labile, internally contradictory, non-monolithic.
>
> (Eagleton 1986: 19)

Symptomatic reading is still a valuable critical procedure, for Eagleton, insofar as ideology tends to constitute a homogeneous discourse. But insofar as it never succeeds in doing so, he argues, other kinds of analysis are also necessary. This is a directly political point, for Eagleton. Behind the totalizing view of ideology he sees at work in Althusser and Macherey, he discerns the Stalinist politics of the French Communist Party. He says:

> If ideology becomes effectively coterminous with lived experience ... then it seems to be essentially deprived of any political cutting-edge as a concept. It has been removed from the terrain of class struggle.
>
> (Eagleton 1982: 55)

In *Walter Benjamin, or Towards a Revolutionary Criticism* (1981), Eagleton moves beyond the Althusserian problematic of his earlier work. He criticizes the very concept of 'Marxist criticism', in whose terms almost all of the major Marxist scholars who analyse literature and art, including Althusser and Macherey, have worked. Most 'Marxist criticism', he argues, has tended to derive from periods of proletarian defeat, and to constitute, from within the institutions of a dominant capitalist society, a theoretical re-working, from the standpoint of historical materialism, of aesthetic categories that are fundamentally alien to that materialism. 'Literature' itself is such a category. Eagleton writes:

> It is certainly possible to produce Marxist analyses of George Eliot. It is even necessary. But any 'Marxist criticism' that defines itself in terms of such analyses has once again failed to make a decisive break with bourgeois ideology. Such a criticism, far from staking out a new theoretical space that may make a practical difference, merely addresses new answers to the same object.
>
> (Eagleton 1981: 97)

Eagleton looks beyond Marxist criticism to what he calls 'revolutionary cultural theory', practice and politics. He finds an example of such a practice in contemporary feminist criticism. Feminist criticism, although often produced in universities, is not detached from a wider political movement; it is aware of the ideological effects of literary texts and of their role within social institutions; indeed, a dominant mode of feminist criticism began by criticizing and reconstructing the literary canon. As a result, it rarely falls into the ideological trap of detaching literary texts from the social context of their production and reception. In these respects, Eagleton argues, revolutionary cultural politics can learn from feminism. He describes the discourse of such a politics as follows:

> It would dismantle the ruling concepts of 'literature', reinserting 'literary' texts into the whole field of cultural practices. It would strive to relate such cultural practices to other forms of social activity, and to transform the cultural appa-

ratuses themselves. It would articulate its cultural analyses with a consistent political intervention. It would deconstruct the received hierarchies of 'literature' and transvaluate received judgements and assumptions; engage with the language and 'unconscious' of literary texts, to reveal their role in the ideological construction of the subject; and mobilize such texts, if necessary by 'hermeneutic violence', in a struggle to transform those subjects within a wider political context.

(Eagleton 1981: 98)

As this passage suggests, Eagleton was also aware of the political significance of the deconstructive criticism associated with the French philosopher Jacques Derrida (1930–2004). Derrida's work was received into American literary studies by a group of critics who used it to explode the textual orthodoxies of New Criticism and emphasize the endless play of signification opened up by literary texts. Disapproving of the continued separation of politics from criticism by this kind of learned hedonism, Eagleton made use of deconstruction, as Derrida himself had intended it, as a politically critical mode of analysis. Eagleton appropriated Derrida's method of analysing the contradictions between a text's apparent purpose and what it does in practice, in order to criticize the logic of ideological discourses in literary, cultural and critical texts. Since the mid-1990s, Eagleton has begun to turn his attention to the politics of Irish history. The kind of cultural politics with which he has sought to displace Marxist literary criticism, then, has consisted of an eclectic blend of Marxism, feminism, deconstruction, post-colonialism and cultural studies, to name only the major discourses on which he draws in continuing Althusser's project in his post-Althusserian way, namely the development of a politically progressive mode of cultural analysis.

## *SCREEN*: CINEMA AND THE SUBJECT

Althusser's ideas were used more freely than by Macherey or Eagleton in the work of a group of critics centred around the journal *Screen* in the 1970s. Published by the Society for Education in Film and Television, from 1971 *Screen* became the leading forum in Britain for theoretical analysis of film, a medium that had been largely ignored by academic literary criticism. The journal's first major influence was the film theory of the French critic Christian Metz, which provided a starting point for a detailed method of film analysis that was indebted to structuralist literary criticism. *Screen* criticized a purely descriptive study of cinematic signs, however, from a Marxist perspective influenced by Althusser. As Colin MacCabe, one of the editors and contributors to *Screen* in this period, wrote:

> Althusser's thought ... provided the intellectual space in which a specific analysis of a cultural form, in this case film and cinema, could be carried out in the conviction that, at a later date, this specificity could be related to the fundamental divisions of capital and labour and the ideological formations which played their part in the reproduction of that division.
>
> (MacCabe 1985: 13)

According to MacCabe, *Screen* made use of two elements of Althusser's work in particular. In the first place, the latter's concept of the relative autonomy of superstructural formations such as cinema allowed the journal's critics to practise a detailed analysis of cinematic forms without having to force these analyses back to the economic situation of these forms until it appeared genuinely relevant to do so. Althusser's work enabled *Screen*'s critics to undertake a materialist and socialist analysis of cinema free from the economic determinism of an earlier generation of Marxist criticism. In the second place, MacCabe writes, the concept of relative autonomy allowed these critics to take seriously the effect of political interventions within their own institutions and disciplines. To argue for a materialist analysis of film, for example, in institutions traditionally devoted to humanistic appreciation of 'English Literature' was, in the light of Althusser's work, a struggle indirectly but ultimately related to class struggle in the society of which that institution was a part. Put simply, he writes, 'Althusser enabled one to take institutions and ideas seriously while still genuinely retaining a belief in the reality of class struggle and revolution' (MacCabe 1985: 16).

*Screen*'s most important contribution to theoretical debate in the 1970s, however, was the attempt made by many of its writers to think through the relationship between the function of cinema in ideology, on the basis of Althusser's work, and its function in the life of the individual subject, on the basis of the psychoanalysis of Jacques Lacan. Althusser had argued that ideology interpellates us as subjects. Lacan also thought of the individual as a 'subject', split by its entry into language, in which its pre-linguistic desire cannot find expression. For Lacan, it is the 'symbolic' order of language and of all the codes, analogous to that of language, by which society functions, that determines the subjectivity of the developing individual. For Althusser, this order can be described primarily as that of ideology. *Screen*'s most valuable work consisted in its contributors' attempts to relate Lacan's account of the individual subject, insofar as it is determined by language, to Althusser's account of the subject, insofar as it is determined by ideology. In 'Anata Mo' (1976), Stephen Heath writes:

> There is a material history of the construction of the individual as subject and that history is also the social construction of the subject; it is not, in other words, that there is first of all the construction of a subject for social/ideological formations and then the placing of that constructed subject-support in those formations, it is that the two processes are one, in a kind of necessary simultaneity – like the recto and verso of a piece of paper.
>
> (Heath 1976: 62)

Heath means that the individual subject is determined by two processes at once, which in reality interact with one another to form a single, complex process. On the one hand, the subject is constantly positioned as such – that is to say, our understanding of ourselves is constantly determined – by the linguistic forms into which we enter as speaking subjects. On the other hand, these forms also mediate class-interests in the society into which we enter at the same time. Language positions us as subjects of desire; ideology positions us as subjects of class society. What is important, for Heath and other contributors to *Screen*, is to analyse the ways in which cinema functions in both processes at once. So, in 'Theory and Film' (1976), for example, Colin MacCabe begins by analysing the relationship between the 'look' and the 'point of view' in *American Graffiti* (George Lucas, 1973). The cinematic devices that construct a stable identity for the film's protagonist, he argues, provide the spectator with a point of view from which he can watch the film as a character with a similarly stable identity. MacCabe relates the construction of this point of view to the pleasure of what Lacan calls the 'imaginary', my misunderstanding of myself as a stable unity, of which I am in control. Various 'looks' in the film, according to MacCabe, threaten to disrupt this security, but its narrative and cinematic devices function to resolve these threats. MacCabe then goes on to argue that 'the breaking of the imaginary relation between text and viewer is the first requisite of political questions in art' (MacCabe 1985: 73). As *American Graffiti* functions to preserve a stable subject position from which it can be watched, MacCabe argues, so it removes its viewer from the social contradictions in which such a position is in reality an ideological illusion. Specifically, removes its American viewers from the context of the impact of the Vietnam war within which they are really watching it in 1973. The subject position constructed for the viewer by the film is one of knowledge – it is from a position of knowledge that we look back at the innocence of the pre-Vietnam age it portrays as such. As MacCabe writes, 'this knowledge presupposes us outside politics now, outside contradiction' (MacCabe 1985: 73). This constitutes what Althusser calls an imaginary representation of our real relationship to our conditions of existence. The film, MacCabe argues, allowed its first viewers to live an ideological relationship to the complex set of contradictions that constituted American society in the era of the Vietnam war. At the same time as this, and in the very same process, he argues, it provides them as individual subjects with the pleasurable reassurance of an ultimately stable identity, in the face of the many threats to such an identity that continually impinge upon the individual from the unconscious.

## RAYMOND WILLIAMS: CULTURAL MATERIALISM

*Screen*'s writers are clearly beginning to move beyond the terms of Althusser's own work. However, the most influential move beyond the problematic of Althusser's work in literary and cultural studies has been the 'cultural materialism' developed by Raymond Williams

(1921–1988). In *Marxism and Literature* (1977), Williams moves specifically beyond the theory of ideology in whose terms Althusser and Althusserian critics analysed literary and cultural works. As opposed to the theory of ideology, he argues for the greater value in cultural interpretation of the concept of 'hegemony', developed by the Italian Communist Antonio Gramsci (1891–1937). In the notebooks written during his imprisonment under Mussolini, Gramsci distinguishes hegemony from 'rule', or the direct coercion used in times of crisis by the ruling class or class-alliance to maintain its position as such. Hegemony, on the other hand, is the more usual complex of political, social and cultural forces which work to promote a consensus in society that the current system of social relations is the 'natural', inevitable, or the best realistically possible system. The advantage, for Williams, of this concept over the traditional Marxist concept of ideology is that it situates the process of domination at work in cultural forms at the level of the *whole process* of social life rather than simply at the level of conscious ideas, beliefs and systems of thought. He writes:

> Hegemony is then not only the articulate upper level of 'ideology', nor are its forms of control only those ordinarily seen as 'manipulation' or 'indoctrination'. It is a whole body of practices and expectations, over the whole of living: our senses and assignments of energy, our shaping perceptions of ourselves and the world. It is a lived system of meanings and values – constitutive and constituting – which as they are experienced as practices appear as reciprocally confirming.
>
> (Williams 1977: 110)

Although Williams mentions Althusser's work as a variation on the traditional Marxist theme of ideology as a 'conscious system of ideas and beliefs', this definition of hegemony cannot be contrasted with Althusser's concept of ideology. This passage is just as faithful an account of Althusser's concept of ideology as it is of Gramsci's concept of hegemony. Williams even uses one of the former's key terms, 'lived'. Where Williams is able to use Gramsci's concept genuinely to move beyond Althusser is in the concepts of 'counter-hegemony' and 'alternative hegemony'.

Althusser by no means reduces the concept of ideology to that of the ideology of the ruling class. In 'Theory, Theoretical Practice and Theoretical Formation' he speaks of 'different ideological tendencies' that represent the positions of different social classes. This is the sense in which we can speak of proletarian as well as of bourgeois ideology. In the ISAs essay, Althusser makes clear that ISAs are not themselves ideologies, but rather 'the *site* of class struggle' in which oppositional ideologies can find space to articulate their resistance to the dominant ideology. Nevertheless, the emphasis in Althusser's thought is clear. While there are oppositional ideologies, and institutions in which these find expression, they are nevertheless largely neutralized as an effective form of social resistance by incorporation into the dominant ideology and its institutions. In Williams's view, this is to underemphasize the role played in the complex whole of social life by cultural forms, ideas and energies that resist, oppose or break from the dominant ideologies. Like Gramsci, he argues that in any social process, whilst there are hegemonic forms and discourses at work whose function is ultimately to maintain the existing structure of class relations, there is nevertheless also a significant complex of 'counter-hegemonic' forms and discourses, which work against this structure. Williams writes:

> The reality of any hegemony, in the extended political and cultural sense, is that, while by definition it is always dominant, it is never either total or exclusive. At any time, forms of alternative or directly oppositional politics and culture exist as significant elements in the society.
>
> (Williams 1977: 113)

In terms of historical, political or cultural analysis, Williams argues, the concept of hegemony allows us to understand the complex reality of the mutual relationship between the hegemonic and counter-hegemonic forms of a given social process. The hegemonic forms of a culture – as opposed to the concept of its 'dominant ideology' – are a constant process of response to the discourses and practices that resist, oppose and develop alternatives to them, and their forms and contents are determined by this process. In the same way, counter-hegemonic discourses evolve in forms determined by the hegemonic practices they resist. Williams writes:

> Any hegemonic process must be especially alert and responsive to the alternatives and opposition which question or threaten its dominance. The reality of cultural process must then always include the efforts and contributions of those who are in one way or another outside or at the edge of the terms of the specific hegemony.
>
> (Williams 1977: 113)

Williams develops a terminology with which to analyse the 'internal dynamic relations of any actual process' of social life. In the first place, he argues, we need to maintain the concept of 'dominant' or hegemonic cultural forms and practices. In the complex reality of any given social process, however, Williams argues that these dominant forms and practices function in a mutually determining relationship with what he calls 'residual' and 'emergent' forms. In the first place, he distinguishes the residual elements of a cultural process from the merely 'archaic', which is 'wholly recognized as an element of the past', to be observed and even from time to time consciously 'revived' as such. In British culture, the monarchy is such an archaic element. The residual, on the other hand, is that which has been developed in the past, but which is 'still active in the cultural process, not only and often not at all as an element of the past, but as an effective element of the present' (Williams 1977: 122). Residual elements of a cultural process, that is, are past forms of life that still constitute an active force in the culture of the present. One of Williams' example of such a form in British culture is organized Christianity. He distinguishes between those residual forms that have been incorporated into the dominant culture and those that oppose or present an alternative to it. So within the church, as it functions in contemporary culture, there are meanings and values, such as official morality or social order, that have become incorporated into the dominant culture, but others, such as absolute equality or service without reward, that constitute an alternative to it. By the 'emergent',

Williams means first the 'new meanings and values, new practices, new relationships and kinds of relationship' that are continually being created in the process of social life. It is important – and in practice, difficult – he argues, to distinguish here between forms that are merely elements of a new phase of the dominant culture, and genuinely emergent forms, which represent the development of an alternative way of social life altogether. A new social class will develop emergent cultural forms, Williams argues, as the working class has done since its formation in the Industrial Revolution. These forms are typically developed unevenly in relation to the dominant cultural practices that arise in response to them in a 'process of attempted incorporation' into the dominant culture. Emergent practices are not only the product of an oppositional social class, however. Williams argues that no dominant culture ever includes or incorporates every aspect of human thought and practice. Indeed, he writes, dominant cultures can be historically compared on the basis of the extent to which they incorporate the range of practices within the culture that they dominate. For Williams, it is typically 'the personal or the private', 'the natural or even the metaphysical' that dominant cultural formations tend to exclude – since, by definition, such formations work primarily at the level of the ruling concept of the social. He writes:

> There is always other social being and consciousness [than that which derives from an oppositional class] which is excluded: alternative perceptions of others, in immediate relationship; new perceptions and practices of the material world.
>
> (Williams 1977: 126)

Gay and lesbian cultural forms and practices are an example of an emergent element in contemporary culture, as are gay and lesbian studies within the institution of literary and cultural studies. In practice, Williams argues, it is often difficult clearly to denote such an emergent cultural form as such. Cultural formations also include what he calls 'pre-emergent' forms, or 'structures of feeling'. What he means by these latter terms is this. In any given social process, there are a host of discursive forms available for the expression of the variety of social experience. In practice, however, these forms lag, as it were, behind experience – our lives, thoughts and energies change more quickly than the cultural forms in which we express them. Williams writes: 'Practical consciousness is almost always different from official consciousness' (Williams 1977: 130). A given social group or generation lives differently to the ways in which the culture as a whole says that it is living. Williams writes:

> Yet the actual alternative to the received and produced fixed forms is not silence: not the absence, the unconscious, which bourgeois culture has mythicized. It is a kind of feeling and thinking which is indeed social and material, but each in an embryonic phase before it can become fully articulate and defined exchange.
>
> (Williams 1977: 131)

This is what Williams means by a 'pre-emergent' 'structure of feeling'. Before new social energies, goals and values can be given a fully articulate or systematic form of expression, less articulate and systematic forms arise. This can be seen in new *styles* – of speech, manners, dress and so on – as well as in new artistic forms. The point for Williams is that a present set of lived concerns, for which the current cultural process has no adequate forms of expression, is coming to articulation within that culture. Hence he writes:

> Structures of feeling can be defined as social experience *in solution*, as distinct from other social semantic formations which have been *precipitated* and are more evidently and more immediately available.
>
> (Williams 1977: 133)

Williams is an appropriate figure with which to conclude this chapter, inasmuch as he exemplifies the way in which Althusser has continued to be influential in literary and cultural studies from the theory revolution of the 1970s up to the present day. Williams's own work has been highly influential in literary studies, in which cultural materialism continues to be a dominant discourse, as it has been in cultural studies, of which he is usually regarded as one of the founders.

*Influenced himself* by Althusser's work in the 1970s, that is, Williams has influenced the development of many contemporary forms of politically committed criticism. In this, his work typifies the continuing presence of Althusser in literary and cultural studies. Although there are few card-carrying Althusserian critics today, nevertheless almost every form of political criticism is indebted, to some extent, to his work, through his influence on political criticism since the 1970s. New Historicism, cultural materialism, post-colonial and race-oriented criticism, gay and queer theory, feminism, post-structuralism and cultural studies are all discourses that work within an intellectual horizon of which Althusser's work is an essential part, especially his theory of ideology. Althusser thus remains a critical thinker for cultural critics today, inasmuch as the discourses within literary studies which aim truly to *criticize* the global capitalist society within which they are practised are formulated within a frame of reference which his work has shaped. You can neither understand nor practise political criticism today without coming to terms – whatever those terms may be – with Althusser.

# FURTHER READING

## WORKS BY ALTHUSSER

For a list of abbreviations used in references to Althusser's work throughout this book, please see the Works Cited section. Works listed only in French are currently unavailable in English translation.

Althusser, L. (1969) *For Marx*, trans. B. Brewster, London and New York: Verso. First published as *Pour Marx*, Paris: Maspero, 1965
Althusser's first major collection of essays. 'Marxism and Humanism' contains his first discussion of ideology, and the essay on Bertolazzi and Brecht puts the concept to work in theatre criticism.

Althusser, L. and Balibar, É. (1970) *Reading Capital*, trans. B. Brewster, London and New York: Verso. First published as *Lire le Capital*, Paris: Maspero, 1968.
In the first section, Althusser outlines the concept of symptomatic reading. In the second, he reads the fundamental concepts of the Marxist science of history out of *Capital*. For the full French text, see *Lire le Capital*, vols. 1 and 2, Paris: Maspero, 1965.

Althusser, L. (1971) *Lenin and Philosophy, and Other Essays*, trans. B. Brewster, London: New Left Books, and New York: Monthly Review Press.

In these essays, Althusser develops his 'second definition' of philosophy, as the 'class struggle in theory'. See especially 'Lenin and Philosophy' (1968), and the interview 'Philosophy as a Revolutionary Weapon' (1967). This collection also contains the 1969 essay on Ideological State Apparatuses, the letter on art (1966) and the essay on Cremonini's painting (1966).

Althusser, L. (1976) *Essays in Self-Criticism*, trans. G. Lock, London: New Left Books, and Atlantic Highlands, NJ: Humanities Press.
Revisions of the positions of *For Marx* and *Reading Capital*. The 1972 'Reply to John Lewis' redefines philosophy as class struggle in theory.

Althusser, L. (1977). 'On the Twenty-Second Congress of the French Communist Party', trans. B. Brewster, *New Left Review*, 104: 3-22.
The first of Althusser's increasingly critical commentaries on the theory and practice of the French Communist Party.

Althusser, L. (1978) 'The Crisis of Marxism', trans. G. Lock, *Marxism Today*, July 1978: 215-20, 227.
Althusser's controversial account of the serious problems in contemporary Marxist theory and practice.

Althusser, L. (1978). 'What Must Change in the Party', trans. P. Camiller, *New Left Review*, 109: 19-45.
An angry exposé, originally published in *Le Monde*, of the theoretical and practical errors in the French Communist Party that led to the defeat of the Union of the Left in the French elections of 1978.

Althusser, L. (1983) 'Appendix: Extracts from Althusser's *Note on the ISAs*', trans. J. Leaman, *Economy and Society* 12: 455–67.
Althusser returns to the issues raised in 'Ideology and Ideological State Apparatuses' in a 1976 text unpublished in French during his lifetime.

Althusser, L. (1990) *Philosophy and the Spontaneous Philosophy of the Scientists, and Other Essays*, ed. G. Elliott, London and New York: Verso.
The first essay contains an important section on ideology. The 1967 title essay represents the turning point between *For Marx* and *Reading Capital*, and the second definition of philosophy as the class struggle in theory.

Althusser, L. (1993) *The Future Lasts a Long Time: A Memoir*, ed. O. Corpet and Y.M. Boutang, trans. R. Veasey, London: Chatto and Windus. First published as *L'avenir dure longtemps*, suivi de *Les faits*, Paris: Stock/IMEC, 1992.

Highly readable. Althusser's account of his psychological development, written in place of the testimony he would have given in court concerning his wife's murder. Also contains the 1976 autobiographical fragment, *The Facts*.

Althusser, L. (1994a) *Écrits philosophiques et politiques,* vol. 1, ed. F. Matheron, Paris: Stock/IMEC.

'Louis Althusser après Althusser' is of particular interest, containing texts written after Althusser's hospitalization in 1980. 'Le courant souterrain du matérialisme de la rencontre' (1982) introduces the concept of aleatory materialism.

Althusser, L. (1994b) *Sur la philosophie*, Paris: Gallimard.

The post-1980 interviews and correspondence with Fernanda Navarro on aleatory materialism.

Althusser, L. (1995a) *Écrits philosophiques et politiques*, vol. 2, ed. F. Matheron, Paris: Stock/IMEC.

Includes Althusser's untranslated essays on theatre and art, 'Écrits sur l'art'.

Althusser, L. (1995b) *Sur la reproduction*, Paris: Presses Universitaires de France.

The complete text of the previously unpublished work from which Althusser extracted 'Ideology and Ideological State Apparatuses'.

Althusser, L. (1996) *Writings on Psychoanalysis: Freud and Lacan*, ed. O. Corpet and F. Matheron, trans. J. Mehlman, New York: Columbia University Press. An abridged translation of *Écrits sur la psychanalyse: Freud et Lacan*, Paris: Stock/IMEC, 1993.

An important complement to Althusser's philosophical work, making clear his detailed interest in psychoanalysis.

Althusser, L. (1997) *The Spectre of Hegel: Early Writings*, ed. F. Matheron, trans. G. Goshgarian, London and New York: Verso. A translation of Part 1 of *Écrits philosophiques et politiques*, vol. 1, Paris: Stock/IMEC, 1994.

Early works, from 1946–53. Throws light on the complex development of Althusser's mature positions from his early Hegelianism, Catholicism and Stalinism.

Althusser, L. (1998a) *Lettres à Franca, 1961–1973*, Paris: Stock/IMEC.

A selection of letters written to Althusser's lover during the period of his most influential work. Contains many reflections on this work and on contemporary philosophy and culture.

Althusser, L. (1998) *Solitude de Machiavel, et autres texts*, ed. Y. Sintomer, Paris: Presses Universitaires de France.

The discussion following Althusser's presentation of 'Lenin and Philosophy' to the Société Française de Philosophie is of particular interest.

The reader should also consult Balibar's later reflections on his contribution to *Reading Capital*:

Balibar, É. (1973) 'Self-Criticism: Answer to Questions from "Theoretical Practice"', *Theoretical Practice* 7–8: 56–72.

# MARX

Marx, K. (1964) *The Economic and Philosophical Manuscripts of 1844*, ed. D. Struik, trans. M. Milligan, New York: International.

Written 1844, first published in German in 1932. The first draft of the systematic study of economics that occupied Marx throughout his life. The key text of the 'young Marx', and the basis of all subsequent Marxist humanism. The most important chapter is 'Estranged Labour'.

Marx, K. and Engels, F. (1976) *The German Ideology*, in *Collected Works*, vol. 5: *Marx and Engels 1845–47*, London: Lawrence and Wishart, and New York: International.

Written 1845, first published in German in 1932. Read the Preface and Section 1, 'Feuerbach' (about 70 pages). Marx and Engels' most systematic account of the materialist conception of history.

Marx, K and Engels, F. (2002) *The Communist Manifesto*, ed. G. Stedman Jones, trans. S. Moore, London and New York: Penguin.
First published in German in 1848. A short and accessible introduction. Recounts the history of the class struggles leading to that of the bourgeoisie and the proletariat.

Marx, K. (1977) 'Preface to *A Critique of Political Economy*', in *Selected Writings*, ed. D. McLellan, Oxford and New York: Oxford University Press.
First published in German in 1859. An account in two or three pages of Marx's intellectual development, and a concise exposition of the materialist conception of history.

Marx, K (1976), *Capital: A Critique of Political Economy,* vol. 1, trans. B. Fowkes, Harmondsworth and New York: Penguin.
First published in German in 1867. Although initially technical, it is quite comprehensible. The key text with which Althusser negotiates. It is a long work, which repays reading in full. An introductory selection, of more accessible length, can be found in *Karl Marx: Selected Writings*, ed. D. McLellan (Oxford and New York: Oxford University Press, 1977).

Marx, K. and Engels F. (1976) *On Literature and Art*, Moscow: Progress.
Marx and Engels' occasional pieces on literature and art. Most interesting are Marx's fragment on Greek art, and the letters of Marx and Engels to the socialist authors Minna Kautsky, Margaret Harkness and Ferdinand Lassalle.

## WORKS ON ALTHUSSER

Works listed only in French are unavailable in English translation.

Albiac, G. *et al.* (1997) *Lire Althusser aujourd'hui*, Paris: L'Harmattan.
On Althusser's corpus as redefined by the posthumous publications and scholarship. Marc Howlett analyses Althusser's concept of theatre.

Boutang, Y.M. (1992) *Louis Althusser: une biographie*, vol. 1: *La formation du mythe (1918–1956)*, Paris: Grasset.
The meticulously researched first volume of Althusser's biography. Regrettably still untranslated, it is nevertheless essential, and worth reading as much as your French allows.

Callari, A. and Ruccio, D., eds. (1998) *Rereading Althusser*: special issue of *Rethinking Marxism*, 10/3.

An important collection, whose analyses include the posthumous works. François Matheron analyses the concept of the void in Althusser; Max Statkiewicz examines Althusser's concept of theatre, based on two of the posthumous essays; Fernanda Navarro gives the clearest account in English of Althusser's work after 1980; Gabriel Albiac reads *The Future Lasts a Long Time*.

Elliott, G. (1987) *Althusser: The Detour of Theory*, London and New York: Verso.

The best study in English. Invaluable material on the political and philosophical contexts of Althusser's interventions.

Elliott, G., ed. (1994) *Althusser: A Critical Reader*, Oxford and Cambridge, MA: Blackwell.

A collection of major critical essays. Especially valuable are: Eric Hobsbawm's early review, Paul Ricoeur on ideology, Francis Mulhern on Althusser's influence in literary studies, and Gregory Elliott's study of *The Future Lasts a Long Time*. Peter Dews on the epistemological context and David Macey on Althusser's relation to Lacan are also informative.

Goldstein, P., ed. (1994) *The Legacy of Althusser*: special issue of *Studies in Twentieth Century Literature*, 18/1.

Some literary readings of Althusser's contemporary significance. Chip Rhodes's argument that mass culture is now the dominant ISA is especially worthwhile. David Margolies gives an account of 'Althusserianism' in literary studies.

Kaplan, E. A. and Sprinker, M., eds. (1993) *The Althusserian Legacy*, London and New York: Verso.

An early and wide-ranging symposium on Althusser's significance in the human sciences. Étienne Balibar reflects critically on Althusser's concept of ideology, and Warren Montag gives an important account of the 'Spinozism' of Althusser's theory of reading. Also contains a useful interview with Jacques Derrida on his former colleague.

Lezra, J., ed. (1995) *Depositions: Althusser, Balibar, Macherey, and the Labor of Reading*: special issue of *Yale French Studies*, 88.
Some advanced philosophical and critical studies. Judith Butler negotiates with the ISAs essay; Ellen Rooney analyses Althusser's theory of reading.

Montag, W. (2003) *Louis Althusser*, Houndmills and New York: Palgrave Macmillan.
Contains a critical defence of Althusser's and Macherey's literary theory, and a symptomatic reading of *The Future Lasts a Long Time*. Includes a translation of Althusser's essay, 'On Brecht and Marx'.

Thompson, E.P. (1978), 'The Poverty of Theory: or an Orrery of Errors', in *The Poverty of Theory, and Other Essays*, London: Merlin, and New York: Monthly Review Press.
A historian's polemic against Althusser's 'Stalinism'.

# ALTHUSSERIAN LITERARY THEORY AND CRITICISM

These are some of the main works of literary theory and criticism in which the significance of Althusser's work in these disciplines is worked out:

Balibar, É. and Macherey, P. (1996) 'On Literature as an Ideological Form', in T. Eagleton and D. Milne, eds., *Marxist Literary Theory: A Reader*, Oxford and Cambridge, MA: Blackwell. First published as 'Préface', in R. Balibar, *Les français fictifs*, Paris: Hachette, 1974.
A revision of Macherey's earlier theory in the light of the ISAs essay. On the constitution and role of literature within the French educational ISA.

Balibar, R. (1974) *Les français fictifs: Le rapport des styles littéraires au français national*, Paris: Hachette.
An analysis of the function of literary language in the French educational ISA.

Balibar, R. (1978) 'An Example of Literary Work in France: George Sand's "La Mare au Diable" / "The Devil's Pool" of 1846', in F. Barker et al., *1848: The Sociology of Literature*, Colchester: University of Essex Press.

An English introduction to Renée Balibar's work on class conflict in national and literary language in the light of Althusser's theory of the educational ISA.

Bennett, T. (2003) *Formalism and Marxism*, 2nd edition, London and New York: Routledge.
A critique of the idealist concept of 'literature' at work in Althusserian aesthetics.

Eagleton, T. (1976) *Criticism and Ideology: A Study in Marxist Literary Theory*, London and New York: Verso.
A dense study in Marxist literary theory, influenced by Althusser and Macherey, whom Eagleton nevertheless criticizes and attempts to move beyond, especially in the final chapter on aesthetic value.

Eagleton, T. (1981) *Walter Benjamin, or Towards a Revolutionary Criticism*, London: Verso.
The preface and the chapter on 'Marxist Criticism' mark Eagleton's development beyond the Althusserian problematic of Marxist literary theory. The second section exemplifies the new position.

Eagleton, T. (1986) *Against the Grain: Essays 1975–1985*, London: Verso.
The chapter on Conrad's *The Secret Agent* exemplifies Eagleton's Althusserian criticism. The chapter on Macherey critically reviews *A Theory of Literary Production* and two later essays. In the preface, Eagleton settles accounts with his former Althusserian positions.

Feltes, N. (1986) *Modes of Production of Victorian Novels*, Chicago and London: University of Chicago Press.
An Althusserian account of the ways in which five Victorian novels are determined by the changing modes of literary production within the capitalist social formation.

Feltes, N. (1993) *Literary Capital and the Late Victorian Novel*, Madison: University of Wisconsin Press.
A development of the previous book. Feltes analyses the distinct practices which constitute the late Victorian publishing industry, and argues that a series of novels and essays are determined by these practices.

Jameson, F. (1981) *The Political Unconscious: Narrative as a Socially Symbolic Act*, London: Routledge.
A theory of narrative and its relation to the history of class struggles, which engages with Althusser's concept of structural causality.

Macherey, P. (1976) 'The Problem of Reflection', trans. S. Lanser, *Substance* 15: 6–20.
Macherey's most mature 'Althusserian' statement. A critical development of the traditional concept of Marxist aesthetics, arguing for an analysis of literature *both* as an ideological form and as a process of production.

Macherey, P. (1978) *A Theory of Literary Production*, trans. G. Wall, London and New York: Routledge. First published as *Pour une théorie de la production littéraire*, Paris: Maspero, 1966.
The classic work of Althusserian literary theory and criticism. Not easy. Begin with the essay 'Lenin as Critic of Tolstoy', which is the clearest, and also the point of departure for the whole theory. It is worth reading Jules Verne's *The Mysterious Island* before tackling the central essay on Verne.

Macherey, P. (1995) *The Object of Literature*, trans. D. Macey, Cambridge: Cambridge University Press. First published as *À quoi pense la littérature: exercices de philosophie littéraire*, Paris: Presses Universitaires de France, 1990.
A collection of Macherey's literary studies of the 1980s, based on the new concept of 'literary philosophy'.

Macherey, P. (1998) *In a Materialist Way*, ed. W. Montag, trans. T. Stolze, London and New York: Verso.
Contains Macherey's 1991 defence of his *oeuvre*, in which he gives an account of the place of *A Theory of Literary Production* and *The Object of Literature*. 'For a Theory of Literary Reproduction' broaches the question of reception history. The introduction throws light on the relationship between Althusser and Macherey.

Sprinker, M. (1987) *Imaginary Relations: Aesthetics and Ideology in the Theory of Historical Materialism*, London and New York: Verso.
The major American work of Althusserian literary theory. A defence and development of Althusser's aesthetics, which also defends the critical value of deconstruction.

Williams, R. (1977) *Marxism and Literature*, Oxford: Oxford University Press.

The classic statement of the post-Althusserian problematic of 'cultural materialism'.

# WORKS CITED

The following abbreviations have been used:

## WORKS BY LOUIS ALTHUSSER

'CM'  'The Crisis of Marxism', trans. G. Lock, *Marxism Today*, July 1978: 215–20, 227.

ESC  *Essays in Self-Criticism*, trans. G. Lock, London: New Left Books, and Atlantic Highlands, NJ: Humanities Press, 1976.

FLLT  *The Future Lasts a Long Time: A Memoir*, ed. O. Corpet and Y.M. Boutang, trans. R. Veasey, London: Chatto and Windus, 1993.

FM  *For Marx*, trans. B. Brewster, London and New York: Verso, 1969.

LP  *Lenin and Philosophy, and Other Essays*, trans. B. Brewster, London: New Left Books, and New York: Monthly Review Press, 1971.

PSPS  *Philosophy and the Spontaneous Philosophy of the Scientists, and Other Essays*, ed. G. Elliott, trans. B. Brewster et al., London and New York: Verso, 1990.

RC  L. Althusser and É. Balibar, *Reading Capital*, trans. B. Brewster, London: New Left Books, 1970.

'WMCP' 'What Must Change in the Party', trans. P. Camiller, *New Left Review* 109 (1978): 19–45.

## WORKS BY KARL MARX

C  *Capital: A Critique of Political Economy*, vol. 1, trans. B. Fowkes, Harmondsworth and New York: Penguin, 1976.

EPM  *Economic and Philosophical Manuscripts of 1844*, ed. D. Struik, trans. M. Milligan, New York: International, 1964.

G  *Grundrisse: Foundations of the Critique of Political Economy (Rough Draft)*, trans. M. Nicolaus, Harmondsworth: Penguin, and New York: Random House, 1973.

SW  *Selected Writings*, ed. D. McLellan, Oxford and New York: Oxford University Press, 1977.

## WORKS BY KARL MARX AND FRIEDRICH ENGELS

CM  *The Communist Manifesto*, ed. G. Stedman Jones, trans. S. Moore, London and New York: Penguin, 2002.

GI  *The German Ideology*, in *Collected Works*, vol. 5: *Marx and Engels 1845–47*, London: Lawrence and Wishart, and New York: International, 1976.

SC  *Selected Correspondence*, Moscow: Foreign Languages Publishing House, n.d.

## OTHER WORKS

Albiac, G. (1998) 'Althusser, Reader of Althusser: Autobiography as Fictional Genre', trans. C. Campbell, *Rethinking Marxism* 10/3: 80–89.

Balibar, É. and Macherey, P. (1982) 'Interview', *Diacritics* 12: 46–51.

——(1996) 'On Literature as an Ideological Form', in T. Eagleton and D. Milne, eds., *Marxist Literary Theory: A Reader*, Oxford and Cambridge, MA: Blackwell.

Belsey, C. (1980) *Critical Practice*, London and New York: Routledge.

Bennett, T. (2003) *Formalism and Marxism*, 2nd edition, London and New York: Routledge.

Brecht, B. (1964) *Brecht on Theatre: The Development of an Aesthetic*, ed. and trans. J. Willett, London: Methuen, and New York: Hill and Wang.

Communist Party of the Soviet Union (CPSU) (1961) *The Road to Communism: Documents of the 22nd Congress of the Communist Party of the Soviet Union*, Moscow: Foreign Languages Publishing House.

Eagleton, T. (1976) *Criticism and Ideology: A Study in Marxist Literary Theory*, London and New York: Verso.

——(1981) *Walter Benjamin, or Towards a Revolutionary Criticism*, London: Verso.

——(1982) 'Interview', *Diacritics* 12: 53–64.

——(1986) *Against the Grain: Essays 1975–1985*, London: Verso.

——(1988) *Myths of Power: A Marxist Study of the Brontës*, 2nd edition, Basingstoke: Macmillan.

Elliott, G. (1987) *Althusser: The Detour of Theory*, London and New York: Verso.

——(1994), 'Analysis Terminated, Analysis Interminable: The Case of Louis Althusser', in G. Elliott (ed.) *Althusser: A Critical Reader*, Oxford and Cambridge, MA: Blackwell.

Ephron, N., dir. (1998). *You've Got Mail*, Warner Bros.

Fox, E. (1992) 'Madness, Marxism and Murder', *Independent Magazine*, 11 July.

Hawthorne, N. (1983) *The Scarlet Letter*, ed. N. Baym, New York: Penguin (originally published 1850).

Heath, S. (1976) 'Anata Mo', *Screen* 17: 49–66.

Hobsbawm, E. (1994) 'The Structure of *Capital*', in G. Elliott (ed.), *Althusser: A Critical Reader*, Oxford and Cambridge, MA: Blackwell.

Jameson, F. (1991) *Postmodernism, or, The Cultural Logic of Late Capitalism*, London and New York: Verso.

Laclau, E. and Mouffe, C. (2001) *Hegemony and Socialist Strategy: Towards a Radical Democratic Politics*, 2nd edition, London and New York: Verso.

MacCabe, C. (1985) *Theoretical Essays: Film, Linguistics, Literature*, Manchester: Manchester University Press.

Macherey, P. (1977) 'An Interview with Pierre Macherey', *Red Letters* 5: 3–9.

——(1978) *A Theory of Literary Production*, trans. G. Wall, London and New York: Routledge.

——(1995) *The Object of Literature*, trans. D. Macey, Cambridge and New York: Cambridge University Press.

Montag, W. (2003) *Louis Althusser*, Basingstoke and New York: Palgrave Macmillan.

Mulhern, F. (1994) 'Message in a Bottle: Althusser in Literary Studies', in G. Elliott (ed.) *Althusser: A Critical Reader*, Oxford and Cambridge, MA: Blackwell.

Navarro, F. (1998) 'An Encounter with Althusser', *Rethinking Marxism* 10/3: 93–98.

Poster, M. (1975) *Existential Marxism in Postwar France: From Sartre to Althusser*, Princeton: Princeton University Press.

Radway, J. (1984) *Reading the Romance: Women, Patriarchy and Popular Literature*, Chapel Hill, NC: University of North Carolina Press.

Saussure, F. de (1959) *Course in General Linguistics*, ed. C. Bally and A. Sechehaye, trans. W. Baskin, New York: Philosophical Library.

Verne, J. (2001) *The Mysterious Island*, ed. A. Evans and W. Butcher, trans. S. Kravitz, Middletown, CT: Wesleyan University Press (originally published 1875).

Williams, R. (1977) *Marxism and Literature*, Oxford and New York: Oxford University Press.

# INDEX

Albiac, G. 118
aleatory materialism 5, 147
alienation 24–5, 26, 30, 52
alienation-effect 103–5, 109
Althusser, H. *See* Rytmann, H.
Althusser, L.: aesthetics of 6, 95–109, 129–31, 149, 150; life of 2–4, 111–5, 149; mental illness of 4, 111–12; murder of wife 4, 6, 111–3; religion of 2–4; psychology of 113–15, 116; self-criticism of 4, 5, 69, 146; relationship to structuralism 32–3; theory of knowledge of 52–5, 58–9, 73, 76, 95–8; on the young Marx 34–6, 49. *See also* aleatory materialism, class struggle in theory, epistemological break, overdetermination, practice, problematic, science, symptomatic reading
Althusser, L., works of: 'On Brecht and Marx' 151; 'Le courant souterrain du matérialisme de la rencontre' 5, 147; 'Cremonini, Painter of the Abstract' 106–9; 'The Crisis of Marxism' 5, 119–20; *Essays in Self-Criticism* 5, 69–72; *The Facts* 115–16; *For Marx* 3, 5, 27, 32, 33–43, 45–7, 69, 70, 75–80, 95–105; 'Freud and Lacan' 117; *The Future Lasts a Long Time* 4, 6, 111–19, 120–2; 'Ideology and Ideological State Apparatuses' 83–91, 125, 139, 147, 151; *Lenin and Philosophy* 5, 79, 80, 83–91, 106–9, 148; 'A Letter on Art' 95–8, 109, 130; 'Marxism and Humanism' 75–9; 'Marxism Today' 5; 'The "Piccolo Teatro": Bertolazzi and Brecht. Notes on a Materialist Theatre' 98–105; *Sur la philosophie* 5; 'Philosophy and the Spontaneous Philosophy of the Scientists' 5; *Reading Capital* 3, 5, 27, 32,

52–9, 69; 'Reply to John Lewis', 70–2; *The Spectre of Hegel* 4, 147–8; 'Theory, Theoretical Practice and Theoretical Formation' 79–80, 139; 'On the 22nd Congress of the French Communist Party' 5; 'What Must Change in the Party' 5, 120
'Althusserianism' 124–5, 150
*American Graffiti* 136–7
art 15, 95–8, 106–9, 129–31, 149

Bachelard, G. 37
Balibar, É. 11, 124, 125–8, 148, 150, 151
Barthes, R. 32
base and superstructure 15, 26, 41–6, 76
Baudrillard, J. 122
Bauer, B. 12
Belsey, C. 91–4
Bennett, T. 72–3, 97–8
Bertolazzi, C. 95, 98–103, 104, 109
bourgeoisie 20–2, 71, 80, 94, 98, 100, 128, 130
Brecht, B. 95, 103–5, 109
Brontë sisters 47–9

capitalism 1, 2, 21–2, 23, 24–5, 26, 28, 30, 38, 94, 103, 126
Catholic philosophy 22, 28
Chaplin, C. 1–2
Chomsky, N. 35
class 20–2, 38, 40, 61, 69–73, 80, 126, 128
class struggle in theory 4, 6, 52, 69–73, 74, 146
communism 25, 26, 28, 30, 120–1
Communist Party 1, 3, 4, 28, 119–22; French 28, 29, 69, 119–20, 132, 146; of the Soviet Union 28–30
counter-hegemony 139
Cremonini, L. 95, 106–9
cultural materialism 7, 137–43
cultural studies 7, 98, 133–4, 137, 141–2
culture, popular 1–2, 14–15, 16, 17–18, 19–20, 32, 61, 62, 75, 77, 81–3, 84, 85, 148, 150

Daspre, A. 95
Defoe, D. 65–6, 68
Derrida, J. 134, 150
de-Stalinization 29–30
dialectic 38, 39–40, 101–2
dialectical materialism 29, 38

Eagleton, T. 47–9, 124, 129–34
École normale supérieure 2, 3, 28, 111
Eliot, T.S. 6
Elliott, G. 119
Engels, F. 2, 12, 38, 39, 41–2, 70
Enlightenment 23
Ephron, N. 81
epistemological break 39, 97–8; Marx's 36–9, 49, 72
existentialism 22, 28

feminism 7, 121, 133–4, 143
Feltes, N. 152
Feuerbach, L. 12, 34, 36
film theory 134–7

gay and lesbian studies 7, 141, 143
Gibson, W. 17
Glass, P. 17

Gramsci, A. 138–9
Green Party, the 121
Greimas, A. 32

Heath, S. 136–7
Hegel, G.W.F. 3, 4, 34, 38, 39–40, 42
hegemony 138–40
Herr. M. 17
historical materialism 5, 37, 38, 39–46, 49, 57–8, 60, 62, 76, 96, 98, 105, 106, 133
humanism 22–6, 34, 36–9, 49, 70–2, 75–6, 94, 98, 106–9, 117; Marxist 27–30, 70–2

ideology 2, 6, 15, 16–20, 26, 34, 36, 41, 46, 59–69, 72, 73–4, 75–94, 95–109, 117, 129–34, 136–7, 138–40, 143, 146; material existence of 87–8; interpellates individuals as subjects 88–94, 105, 118–19; literature as an ideological form 125–8
Ideological State Apparatuses 72, 75, 83–91, 92, 94, 95, 105, 118–19, 125–9, 139, 146, 147, 150, 151, 152

Jameson, F. 17–18, 19

Khrushchev, N. 29, 30

labour-power 53–6, 59
Lacan, J. 79, 117–8, 136–7
Leavis, F.R. 6, 123
Lenin, V.I. 34
Lévi-Strauss, C. 31
Lewis, J. 70–2
liberation theology 121

literature 1, 2, 12, 15, 16, 33, 35, 41–2, 43, 46, 47–9, 59–69, 72–4, 84, 91–4, 96–7, 98–105, 125–34, 148, 149
literary criticism 6–7, 16, 17, 26, 31–2, 35, 43–5, 47, 47–9, 59–69, 72–4, 75, 86, 91–4, 95, 97–105, 123–43, 149, 151–4
Lyotard, J.-F. 122

MacCabe, C. 135–7
Macherey, P. 3, 6, 51–2, 59–69, 73–4, 82, 113, 125–34, 151, 153
Marx, K. 6, 11–26, 27, 38, 40–2, 52–9, 73, 103, 104, 109, 120–2; on dialectic 39; early humanism of 22–6, 28, 30, 34. *See also* alienation, base and superstructure, class, communism, materialist conception of history
Marx. K, works of: *Capital* 28, 34, 39, 51, 52–9, 73; *The Communist Manifesto* 18, 19, 20, 21, 22; *Economic and Philosophical Manuscripts* 23, 24–5, 28, 30, 34; *The German Ideology* 12, 13, 16, 18, 23, 36; *The Holy Family* 101; Preface to *A Critique of Political Economy* 15; *Theses on Feuerbach* 23, 36
materialist conception of history 12–22, 23, 26, 36, 37
Merleau-Ponty, M. 23
Metz, C. 135
Montag, W. 119, 150
Mulhern , F. 124

Navarro, F. 4, 5, 147, 150
New Criticism 6, 123, 134
New Historicism 7, 143

overdetermination 41–6, 43–6, 47–9, 70

personalism 22, 28
phenomenology 23, 28
Plath, S. 35, 43–5
post-colonialism 7, 134, 143
post-Marxism 7, 120–2, 123
Poster, M. 30
postmodernism 17–18, 19–20
practice 46–9, 58, 70
problematic 33–6, 39, 47, 49, 57–8
production: forces and relations of 13–16, 18, 21–2, 26, 41, 82, 83, 106–9; literary 47–9, 59–69, 98; mode of 16, 17, 18, 40
proletariat 20–2, 38, 80, 99–103, 128, 133, 141
Propp, V. 32
psychoanalysis 4, 6, 31, 43, 51, 56–7, 79, 112, 116–8, 147
Pynchon, T. 17

queer theory 7, 141, 143

Radway, J. 82
realism 91–4
religion 12, 15, 47, 79, 83, 84–91, 140
revolution 21, 27, 49
Ricoeur, P. 150

*Robinson Crusoe* 65–6, 68
Rochet, W. 69
Rousseau, J.–J. 117
Rytmann H. 4, 111–3

Sartre, J.-P. 23, 28
Saussure, F. 30–1, 35
*Scarlet Letter, The* 93
science 2, 37–9, 49, 70–1, 73, 74, 76, 78, 94, 96–8, 109, 117, 129, 131
*Screen* 134–7
Smith, A. 52–3
Sprinker, M. 153–4
Stalin, J. 28–9, 97, 119
structuralism 30–33
subject, the 88–94, 105, 117–19
Sue, E. 101–2
symptomatic reading 6, 51, 52–9, 63–9, 72, 73, 83, 132, 150, 151

Thompson, E.P. 38, 151
Todorov, T. 32

Verne, J. 63–9, 74, 82
Viola, B. 17

Warhol, A. 17
Williams, R. 137–43

Young Hegelians 12
*You've Got Mail* 81

eBooks – at www.eBookstore.tandf.co.uk

# A library at your fingertips!

eBooks are electronic versions of printed books. You can store them on your PC/laptop or browse them online.

They have advantages for anyone needing rapid access to a wide variety of published, copyright information.

eBooks can help your research by enabling you to bookmark chapters, annotate text and use instant searches to find specific words or phrases. Several eBook files would fit on even a small laptop or PDA.

**NEW:** Save money by eSubscribing: cheap, online access to any eBook for as long as you need it.

## Annual subscription packages

We now offer special low-cost bulk subscriptions to packages of eBooks in certain subject areas. These are available to libraries or to individuals.

For more information please contact webmaster.ebooks@tandf.co.uk

We're continually developing the eBook concept, so keep up to date by visiting the website.

# www.eBookstore.tandf.co.uk